THE L.A. DODGERS

The World Champions of Baseball

BY LOU SAHADI
FOREWORD BY VIN SCULLY

QUILL

New York   1982

Library of Congress Catalog Card Number: 82-80303

ISBN 0-688-01236-1 (pbk)

Printed in the United States of America

First Quill Edition

1 2 3 4 5 6 7 8 9 10

Writing a book under the pressure of such an excruciating deadline could not have been possible without the dedicated efforts of Lou-Anne Smith, Eric Daum, Marian Ciaccia, Brandy Stevens, Gerry Repp and the excellent color photography of Mickey Palmer.

Black and white photos by Wide World Photos and the Los Angeles Dodgers.

CONTENTS

To Riv who has eyes of Dodger
blue . . .
and to Francis Albert, Jilly, Helen and
John . . . blues eyes all. Finally, to
Rocco who kept Lasorda calm in New
York.

FOREWORD

BY VIN SCULLY

For the Los Angeles Dodgers—make that the World Champion Los Angeles Dodgers—1981 will always be remembered as "The Year of the Child" and "Team Comeback." Not just any child, mind you, but a very special young man from south of the border named Fernando Valenzuela.

El Toro, as he was soon to be affectionately called, captured the imagination of Dodger fans the final month of the 1980 season when he did not allow an earned run in 17⅔ innings. He captured their hearts the first two months of the 1981 season.

The 20-year-old lefthander from the tiny hamlet of Etchohuaquila in northwestern Mexico who spoke no English did his talking with his now-famous screwball in winning his first eight major league starts.

By the time Fernando and the regular season finished, he tied a 68-year-old major league record for shutouts by a rookie with eight and led the majors in shutouts and strikeouts (180) and the National League in complete games (11) and innings pitched (192⅓).

So impressed with this youngster were the baseball writers of America, they voted Fernando the National Leauge Cy Young and Rookie of the Year awards, the first time anyone has won both awards in the same year.

Not so coincidental to Fernando's burst upon the major league scene was the Dodgers' lightning start from the gate. They won their first six games and 11 of their first 13 to open a lead that would carry them to the first-half title in the strike-divided season. Speaking of gates, the Dodgers continued as the top drawing card in baseball, setting major league records by hitting the million mark in 22 dates and the two-million plateau in 47.

Fernando, who finished 13–7 with a 2.48 earned run average, was hardly a one-man staff. Burt Hooton (11–6, 2.28), Jerry Reuss (10–4, 2.29) and Bob Welch (9–5, 3.45) combined with Fernando to form the Big Four starters, while Steve Howe (5–3, 2.50, 8 saves) and Dave Stewart (4–3, 2.51, 6 saves) anchored a baby-faced bullpen which grew up fast under fire.

Among the regulars, Dusty Baker (.320 average, 9 homers, 49 RBI) finally garnered a richly-deserved All-Star berth and Gold Glove, while Ron Cey (.288, 13, 50), Pedro Guerrero (.300, 12, 48), Steve Garvey (.283,

1

10, 64 and 945 consecutive games played) and Rick Monday (.315, 11, 25, as a part-time performer) played strong supporting roles.

As for Team Comeback, that monicker was to be earned in three post-season series, culminated by the Dodgers winning their fourth world championship in Los Angeles, their first in 16 years.

First there was the National League Western Division against the Houston Astros, the team that beat the Dodgers in a playoff for the West title in 1980. By losing the first two games in the Astrodome, the Dodgers dug themselves into a seemingly insurmountable hole. No matter. With Hooton, Reuss and Valenzuela doing the pitching and Garvey generating what little offense his team needed, the Dodgers rallied to win the Division Series.

Next up was the National League Championship Series against the Montreal Expos, a team the Dodgers had dominated in regular season play. But after the Expos gained a split in the first two games in Los Angeles and won the opener at Olympic Stadium, the Dodgers found themselves in a familiar position . . . looking up.

Enter Hooton. "Happy," who would be named MVP of the LCS, won his second game of the series and got the Dodgers even and, following a one-day rain delay, Fernando won the clincher, thanks to Monday's dramatic ninth-inning home run off Steve Rogers, giving the Dodgers their third pennant in five years.

Visions of that historic—not to mention hysterical—victory still dancing in their heads, the Dodgers continued their modus operandi in the World Series, bowing to the hated Yankees in the first two games at Yankee Stadium. Yankee fans may have been thinking sweep at this point, but it would be the Dodgers who would accomplish that feat, albeit in six games.

Fernando needed a comeback, what else,

for a 5–4 win in Game 3 to keep the Dodgers alive. The Yankees should have been wary when they jumped to a 4–0 lead in Game 4 as, sure enough, the Dodgers came back to win, 8–7, to even the series. Home runs by Guerrero and Yeager were needed to rally the Dodgers to a 2–1 win in game 5 and a 3–2 edge heading back to the Bronx.

Cey, beaned by Goose Gossage in the eighth inning of Game 5, epitomized the determination that marked this Dodger team by returning to the lineup for Game 6. Still, the Yankees jumped on top before the Dodgers scored eight consecutive runs en route to their only laugher in October.

The Penguin, Guerrero, a budding star who drove in five runs in Game 6, and Yeager shared MVP honors in the series.

Child stars and comebacks—it was that kind of year for the World Champion Los Angeles Dodgers. It was one of the most memorable seasons in baseball history.

PETER O'MALLEY

A large photo hangs behind the imposing wooden desk. It is a photograph of the 1977 Dodgers' opening day line-up. The players, including Tom Lasorda, are outside Dodger Stadium against a background of palm trees. They could easily pass for a tour group on holiday. It means a great deal to Peter O'Malley.

"That picture was on the back page of the sports section," said O'Malley, "but I liked it so much, I had it blown up. The only one who isn't in it now is Don Sutton."

In essence, that 1977 photo represents *his* team.

O'Malley's father, Walter, who had headed the organization since its halcyon Brooklyn days, was striken with cancer in 1976. As he appeared less frequently in the office, Peter began to run the club. Peter had virtually taken control of the Dodgers before his father died in 1979.

The elder O'Malley was a shrewd operator. It was he, in fact, who made baseball into a national game, when, in 1958, he headed a movement that brought major league baseball to the West Coast. It was he who took the beloved Dodgers out of Brooklyn and placed them in Los Angeles. And in 1965, he made his son general manager of the Spokane Dodgers of the Pacific Coast League. It was the beginning of young O'Malley's apprenticeship in the baseball business.

"The people had great hopes," O'Malley remembers. "The manager was Duke Snider. The team was being run by the boss' son. We finished last. But I learned more than if we'd won the pennant—about mechanical baseball things and promoting and selling. I had to sell [advertising] space on our outfield fence after the last-place season. It snows in Spokane and I tramped through the stuff until I'd sold every space but two. It was getting close to opening day. I knocked on more and more doors and said, 'If you don't buy space, we'll have to paint the fence, *Prevent Forest Fires.*' By opening day every space was sold."

It was Peter O'Malley who determined back in 1977 that Lasorda would be the one to replace Walter Alston.

"I've really only known two Dodger managers," says O'Malley. "Walter Alston and now Tom Lasorda."

The 44-year-old O'Malley is one of the most low-keyed owners in baseball. And he is one of the game's most gracious owners. He is practically invisible to his players. He doesn't find it

3

necessary to visit the clubhouse and mingle with them. His appearances can be counted on one hand. He did drop into the clubhouse to console his players after losing the World Series in 1974, 1977 and 1978. Otherwise, he leaves the baseball end to Lasorda and his Vice President of Player Personnel, Al Campanis.

"Tommy knows what I want," O'Malley has said. "There's nothing that I can add. If the team is struggling, I may erupt with Tommy and Al here in my office. But it's here.

"My job is keeping everything together—the baseball administration, the stadium operation. If somebody isn't there to keep it together, it's easy to go off in different directions. And once I make a decision, there's no court of appeals. They may not like my decision, but they know it's final.

"However, negotiating player contracts is the part of the job that I do not enjoy. It's one thing to negotiate TV and advertising contracts. But the players are people I've known and watched. In negotiating a player's contract, you don't want to win because you don't want the player to think he's lost. And then you can't give him everything he wants."

O'Malley is firm but sensitive in his dealings with the players. He encourages a wholesome family-type operation, from the management level to the playing field. Although he doesn't reach out to his players physically, he is accessible to them for private talks and consultations. The players know it, too.

"He is the perfect example of the contemporary young owner with a business mind," says first baseman Steve Garvey. "In the old days, you had baseball men; now, you have businessmen. And he believes in stability. By knowing his people he knows how to motivate them and get the most out of them. With the Dodgers, familiarity breeds success."

O'Malley watches over his Dodger family in his own quiet way. Some 15 years ago, while working under his father's regime, he was informed that Don Newcombe, the star Brooklyn Dodger pitcher of the 1950s, had a serious alcohol problem. Newcombe had hocked his World Series ring and watch at a pawnshop in downtown Los Angeles. Without informing anyone, O'Malley drove down to the pawn shop and bought the two items.

"I'm keeping them," O'Malley informed Newcombe, "for your son."

Several years later, when Newcombe had overcome his problem, O'Malley called Newcombe into his office and hired him as the club's Director of Community Relations. He then opened his desk drawer and looked up at Newcombe.

"Here is your World Series ring and watch," he said.

Then, several years ago, Lou Johnson, another Dodger of the 1960s, had both drinking and drug problems. When Newcombe told O'Malley about it, the Dodger president gave Johnson a job on the team's Community Services staff. Last year, Roy Campanella, star Dodger catcher of the 1950s who has been in a wheelchair for over 20 years following a near-fatal car accident, joined the same staff, at O'Malley's request.

On the success of the L.A. Dodger organization, O'Malley says:

"I've learned that you begin by providing comfort for your fans. Good parking. A nice ballpark. Clean restrooms. Dad was big on the restrooms being clean. Then, when you have the proper setting, you need a competitive team. Add a dash of good promotion."

Baseball could use more owners like Peter O'Malley. . . .

5

TOM LASORDA

The room is unique. It could easily be a movie agent's office. The walls are crowded with photographs, so much so, that the desk seems out of place, an invader in a photo gallery. One wall of photographs is devoted to Frank Sinatra. That's sacred. Another wall is the property of Don Rickles. And, as a reminder that baseball is played in Dodger Stadium, the other two walls are filled with baseball photos and mementos. Tom Lasorda, the gregarious manager of the Dodgers, wouldn't have it any other way.

Lasorda's warm, long-term friendship with Sinatra is reflective of the same innate loyalty which Lasorda has brought to the Dodgers. He has been friends of the world-renowned singer and his close aide Jilly Rizzo ever since he became manager of the Dodgers back in 1977. Oh, they had been friends before but never so close as in recent years. As a tribute to their friendship, Lasorda presented both Sinatra and Rizzo with Dodger jackets and caps which they're said to wear proudly. One of Sinatra's relics on Lasorda's wall is an oil painting of the singer leaning on a bar smoking a cigarette in front of an ashtray bearing the inscription, "My Way." There is still another that stands out from the rest. It's a photograph from one of Sinatra's movies. The singer is standing, shrugging his shoulders in front of a wrecked plane. Prankishly, he's written: "So I blew it, Francis."

While many felt that Lasorda had blown it and lost the World Series to the New York Yankees for the third time in five years, the fun-loving Dodger manager's faith never waned after losing the first two games. In case there was any doubt, Sinatra called him daily in New York to encourage him, assuring Lasorda that he would be there cheering when the Series opened in Los Angeles. It was while dining in New York with another Sinatra associate, Rocco Maselli who owns a jewelry store in the Doral Inn Hotel, on Lexington Ave., that Lasorda reflected in a serious moment about his team's chances.

"The day off will do us good," he quietly said. "The team's tired and has been under a lot of pressure, winning the playoffs the way we did. I'll tell you one thing, Rocco, we're going to win this thing. I have a lot of faith in my ballplayers."

It was an extension of the faith that the Dodger organization had in Lasorda when they picked him to succeed Walter Alston four days before the 1976 season ended. The monk-like Alston had managed the Dodgers his way for 23 years—quietly and with little emotion, if any. It was quite a contrast to Lasorda's style. In his four years as coach under Alston, it was Lasorda who mixed and laughed with the players during their moments of triumph and consoled them in their times of frustration. It was Lasorda, too, who dined with the players after games and socialized with them whenever he could. After nearly three decades in the Dodger organization, Lasorda had paid his dues. The job was indeed his, one that he had been waiting for all those years. He didn't hide his feelings about it when he was officially announced as the manager during a press conference.

"This is the greatest day of my life," Lasorda said. "To be selected as manager of an organization I love so deeply, to wake up and learn that I had inherited a post being vacated by the greatest manager in baseball, is like being presented with the Hope diamond. It only proves that loyalty is a two-way street, that after all the love I've shown the Dodgers all these years, the Dodgers love me a little, too.

"Motivation, communication, that's what the job is all about. I want to be like a father to the players, to know their families—everything I can know about them. They need to feel that they have a role, especially guys who aren't playing or the ones who are having a tough time. It's my job to get to them, to make them feel that they're still a part of it. Managing is like holding a dove in your hand. Squeeze too hard and you kill it; not hard enough, and it flies away."

Lasorda, himself, had several opportunities to fly from the Dodger roost in recent years, before his appointment. Three clubs—Pittsburgh, Montreal and Atlanta—had extended managerial offers to Lasorda. He never gave them a thought. He really couldn't.

"I just didn't see myself loving another team," Lasorda explains. "That would be like loving another woman, and I've been married to my wife, Jo, for over 30 years. No, the only team that could make me leave the Dodgers was the Dodgers. If they had ever said they didn't want me to stand in their way, then I would have known they were telling me to go. Of course, they never said I had the job, but they never said I didn't, either. So, I relied on my dedication and loyalty. I told the Dodgers I loved them for 27 years; and when they named me as manager, they said they loved me."

It all began when the Dodgers drafted him out of the Philadelphia Phillies organization in 1945. As a youngster growing up, one of five brothers in an Italian immigrant family in Morristown, Pennsylvania, he dreamed about playing in Yankee Stadium with the Yankees. He figured baseball was his only way out. His father drove a truck to support the family, and he didn't want any part of that. He jokes about it now.

"We were so poor and the soles of my shoes were so thin that I could step on a coin and tell if it was heads or tails," smiles Lasorda.

So when a Phillies' scout offered him $500 to sign a contract to pitch in the minors, he didn't hesitate.

"If he'd only waited fifteen more minutes, I'd have signed and given the scout $500," beamed Lasorda.

In 1950, the Dodgers sent Lasorda to Montreal, their top farm club in those years in the International League. The lefthanded Lasorda pitched well in his five years with the Royals. However, back then, the Brooklyn Dodgers had such luminaries as Carl Erskine, Preacher Roe, Don Newcombe, Russ Meyer, Joe Black, Johnny Podres, and Billy Loes. He couldn't replace any of these. In 1954, however, Lasorda had a strong chance to make the club. Instead, the Dodgers decided to keep another rookie lefthander, Sandy Koufax, and sent Lasorda back to Montreal. In 1956, he had a major league shot with the Kansas City Athletics. After an 0–4 start, Lasorda was returned to Montreal. He ended his minor league career six years later and became a scout for the Dodgers.

"From the day I signed with Montreal, I'd known the Dodger organization was for me," said Lasorda. "I don't know why I wanted to be a Yankee, but I did until the day I joined the Dodgers."

His wife, Jo, vouches for Lasorda's loyalty to the Dodgers all these years. And together they waited until the day when Lasorda would replace Alston. It seemed an eternity.

Lasorda and pitching sensation Fernando Valenzuela.

"Nothing would have hurt us more than his not getting the job," revealed Jo. "We didn't even like to talk about the possibility. We'd always tell ourselves if it didn't happen this year, then it would next year. Every time an offer came from another club, we'd discuss it; but we'd always come to the same conclusion. "If it's not the Dodgers, it's not what Tom wants; and he won't be happy."

Lasorda began his managerial career in 1966. The Dodgers needed a manager for their Ogden, Utah club and asked Lasorda to fill it. Besides being loyal, he was happy to take it. He missed the sounds and the smells of the dugout the years he was scouting. His dream to eventually manage the Dodgers was just beginning. His success was unheard of. He went

to Ogden, Utah, and his team came in first all three years. He was promoted to the Pacific Coast League and, in three years at Spokane, he won a pennant and had second and third place finishes. Before the Dodgers brought him up as a coach in 1973, he led Albuquerque to a pennant in 1972.

Despite his outstanding minor leage success, capturing five pennants in seven seasons, Lasorda's dramatic escapades easily overshadowed his accomplishments. Embracing the father-son image with his players, Lasorda often cajoled them into producing when it was thought not to be possible. Then, too, his fiery Italian temper at times got him into trouble. All of which Lasorda regards as experience— the growing years—towards becoming a major

9

league manager.

His very first season with Ogden, the Dodgers needed a victory on the final day of the schedule to win the Pioneer League pennant. One of his infielders, Gary Wedel, said he couldn't play because he had to attend his uncle's funeral, while an outfielder, Pat Burke, called Lasorda at home and told him he was too sick to play. Lasorda dealt with Wedel first.

"A funeral?" Lasorda asked. "Gary, this is our last game. We're going for a pennant. When was the last time you saw this uncle?"

"Six years ago," answered Wedel.

"What, six years ago?" snapped Lasorda. "If you didn't visit him while he was alive, why should you want to see him now?"

Wedel agreed to play.

Lasorda then went to work on Burke. When the young outfielder called him earlier and reported that he had the flu, Lasorda told him to stay in bed. As the game approached, Lasorda called him from the stadium.

"Listen, son, you don't want to be alone," sighed Lasorda. "Come on out to the clubhouse. We'll put a couple of benches together and you can rest there."

A short while later, Burke arrived in the clubhouse. While the Dodgers were out on the field, Burke made use of the benches Lasorda had set up for him. He hadn't been lying down five minutes when Lasorda walked into the room.

"Come on," encouraged Lasorda, "you don't want to get your clothes wrinkled. Put on your uniform and then lie down."

Like a son obeying his father, Burke did so. As soon as he lay back down, Lasorda came up and told the shocked youngster that he was in the starting lineup.

"But, Skip," began Burke.

"But Skip, nothing," interrupted Lasorda.

The rest was strictly out of Hollywood.

There were two out in the ninth inning with the Dodgers trailing Idaho Falls by one run. Wedel managed to get a walk. That left it all up to Burke. (Wouldn't it be a storybook finish if he could hit a game-winning home run?) Burke did precisely that. The Dodgers won the game and the pennant, and Lasorda began the first of his many victory dances.

Years later at Spokane, Lasorda would of-

Davey Lopes and Bill Russell jog alongside Lasorda during spring training.

ficiate at another of his faith healing sessions. The Spokane Indians had lost six games in a row during Lasorda's second year as manager in 1970. Lasorda felt it was time for a team meeting. Tom Paciorek, an outfielder with the club back then, who later played five years for the Dodgers, remembered it well.

"We expected a real chewing out," recalled Paciorek, "but Tommy was very calm and understanding. He told us these things just happen sometimes in baseball and that we shouldn't worry about them. Then he told us the 1927 Yankees, the greatest team of all time, had lost nine games in a row. The pep talk really picked the club up. We won our next ten games and rolled up the pennant by a mile."

After the season, one of the other players asked Lasorda if the 1927 Yankees really did lose nine consecutive games.

"How the hell should I know?" said Lasorda with a wink.

There is a litany of memories of Lasorda before he finally took over the Dodger fortunes from Alston. Fans in the minors got a glimpse of his temper, one that the Dodgers cautioned him about even before they made

him manager at Ogden in 1966. One incident occurred while he was pitching for Denver in 1956. The Bears were trailing in the championship playoffs, having dropped the first two games of the best-of-seven-series. Ralph Houk, who was the manager of Denver back then, got Lasorda aside and told him it wouldn't be a bad idea to start a fight to wake up the Bears. Lasorda did, and Denver came back to win.

"Actually, Ralph didn't have to ask me because I was thinking the same thing myself," revealed Lasorda.

When he became manager at Ogden, Lasorda had the unflattering distinction of being thrown out of his first five games. The first time occurred in his very first inning as manager. Coaching. at third base, Lasorda caught a foul ball and threw it out of the game. The rival mangaer, Fred Koenig, who was much bigger than Lasorda, came out of the dugout screaming.

"Who the hell are you to do that?" he yelled.

"The ball was dirty," answered Lasorda. "Who the hell are you?"

When Koenig, who was angered by the rookie manager's remarks, came closer to chal-

12

lenge him, Lasorda belted him with a left. Players from both dugouts ran onto the field and a free-for-all erupted.

One winter the Arizona Instructional League learned about Lasorda's temper. At the time, he was the only manager ever ejected from the placid instructional league. He was, in fact, dismissed so often than his players began a pool to pick which inning he would eventually get thrown out. An area scout, Bert Wells, got to the field late one afternoon and was informed that the pool numbers were already gone. Wells broke out with a grin.

"That's fine," he remarked. "I want the chance that says he'll be ejected walking up to the plate with the lineup card."

That was mild. Latin fans in the Caribbean witnessed Lasorda's wrath innumerable times. One winter while managing in the Dominican Republic, Lasorda got ejected during a road game. Infuriated, he took off his shirt and threw it into the stands. He wasn't finished. He then removed the spikes and did the same thing. It wasn't long after that a group of soldiers entered the clubhouse and led him to prison. Lasorda was dumbfounded.

"The general came in and said that I'm not being punished," said Lasorda. "He simply wanted to compliment me for my spirit. He said he wished his team had a manager who did the same."

In fact, in the days before Castro, Lasorda was practically a national hero in Cuba. During the 1953 Winter League World Series, Lasorda admittedly threw a couple of pitches at a hitter. He fired one a third time and hit the batter in the back. The batter got up with vengeance in his eye. Lasorda showed how quickly he could think.

"I thought he was going to first base," recalled Lasorda. "Then I looked up and he was charging me with a bat in his hand. I didn't even have a ball to throw at him, and he was so big there was no use punching him. Just as he started to swing the bat, I threw my glove in his face and tackled him."

Lasorda was lucky to escape with his life. He did such a remarkable job in turning back his bigger challenger that he was cheered by the fans. The very next day, a contingent of Cuban soldiers took him to President Batista.

Lasorda was perplexed.

"He wanted to know if there was anything he could do for me," smiled Lasorda. "I said, 'no, just let me pitch to him again.'"

Lasorda did get the opportunity several days later. He didn't hesitate to knock down the batter again. This time nothing happened.

The Dodgers expected better things to happen when they made him their manager before the 1977 season. The previous two years were futile ones. The Dodgers were clearly outdistanced by the Cincinnati Reds in the Western Division. During that period of frustration, Los Angeles had become noticeably conservative on the field. They really needed someone with Lasorda's fire. They also needed someone with his style. From the very first day of spring training it was evident that Lasorda's refreshing way would become infectious. The business-like handshake was gone. Now it was time for hugging and rah-rah talk. Lasorda could exercise his fatherly philosophy since 16 of the 25 players on the roster had played for him somewhere along the way in the minors.

"When I took this job, they asked me if I was worried about replacing a man who'd had it 23 years," began Lasorda. I told them no, I was worried for the guy who'd have to replace me. I'm the greatest American optimist since General Custer. He was surrounded and outnumbered four-to-one; and he said, 'Don't take any prisoners.'

A slight disagreement with umpire Eric Gregg.

"I try things they say won't work in the majors. Being close to my players, hugging them. They say all players are becoming businessmen, but I managed these guys, some back to Ogden, when they were playing for $500 a month. My clothes are blue, the Dodger color. I won't wear red. Cut my veins and I bleed Dodger blue. If trouble comes, I pray to that Big Dodger in the sky. You know I can't believe it sometimes . . . me being manager of the Dodgers."

The chemistry worked. His very first year in the dugout, the Dodgers were on a Lasorda high. They won 24 of their first 30 games and for all practical purposes the pennant race was over by May. They eventaully won the flag over Cincinnati by ten games. And, to prove that it wasn't a fluke, he won the pennant again in 1978, only to be the second manager in National League history to win a pennant his first two years of managing. He knew it wouldn't be as easy the second time and issued the warning signals when the Dodgers assembled for spring training in 1978.

"We caught them flat a year ago," Lasorda pointed out. "They'll be more prepared this time. I don't think about losing. My father didn't think that way. I try to do everything positive. You saw me pitch. I was a humpty-dumpty. Attitude got me up out of the minor leagues. Attitude. That's the big thing that I had and that I can pass on."

The Dodgers had it that spring. Lasorda keyed it and the players responded. They were a family, a happy family indeed. Lasorda was the father figure. He set the mood as the Dodgers prepared to board their own four-engine jet, one which he calls the largest corporate plane anywhere.

"This is Bill Russell, the best shortstop in the world," Lasorda said. "Not in the National League. The World. Lee Lacy, he can hit with the best of them. His mama told him to make money, but mama never told him how to spend it. That's why he has so much. Right, Lee?"

It was Steve Garvey's turn next.

"Hey, Garve, they tell me you went to an X-rated movie the other night," Lasorda chided. "But you put on a wig and a fake beard so nobody would recognize America's hero."

It was Lasorda at his best. Yet, Rick Monday couldn't wait to retaliate once the plane landed. In the Dodger clubhouse, he spoke in a loud voice to attract any reporters who were around.

"The team is in total disarray," Monday told a reporter. "The only way we stay in shape is running laps around Lasorda. You ought to see him put a full-court press on a smorgasbord. He goes out to speaking dates so much that when he bought a new home, he charged his wife $1,500 to show up at the closing."

Lasorda picked up on the jibe.

"Monday," he shook his head, "you've got eyes like a mullett."

Even before he became manager, Lasorda worked his magic on the Dodger players. While he was still a coach, he used his street smarts to inveigle Joe Ferguson to switch to catcher from playing the outfield. Ferguson didn't relish the idea. First of all he wasn't confident he could do it. Second, he felt he wouldn't get as much recognition catching as he would being an outfielder. Lasorda put his salesmanship to work.

"Mickey Cochrane was one of the greatest catchers who ever lived," he told Ferguson. "Did you know he was a converted outfielder? Lemme tell you something else. Gabby Hartnett was also a great catcher, and did you know he started out as an outfielder. And Ernie Lombardi?"

Ferguson hadn't realized it.

"All three," continued Lasorda, "had not only made the switch successfully but were ultimately elected to the Hall of Fame—as catchers!"

The unsuspecting Ferguson never surmised that all three began as catchers and that Lombardi wasn't found in the Hall of Fame. Some time later, Lasorda was confronted with it. He never flinched.

"I know that and you know that, but Joe Ferguson doesn't know that," Lasorda said without a hint of a smile.

The Dodgers knew that one day Lasorda would ultimately replace Alston, perhaps as early as 1968, although it was too soon then. They had Lasorda's word. He gave them a bigger than life commitment.

14

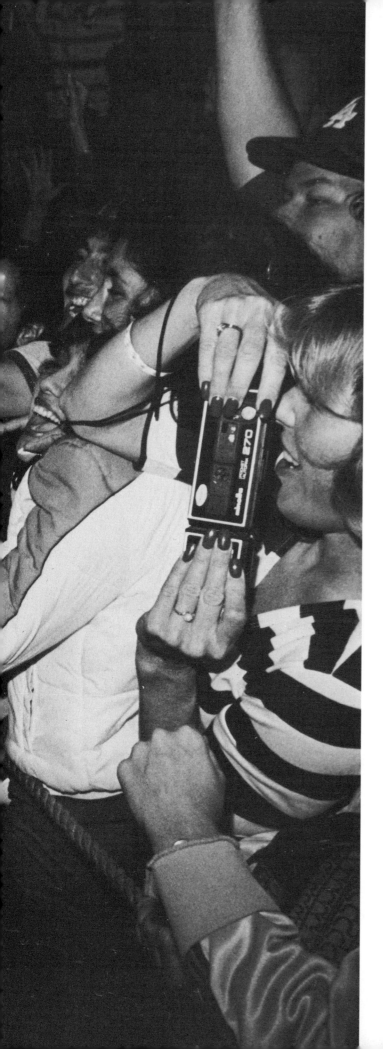

"I told Mr. O'Malley once, that I'd like to work for the Dodgers after I'm dead and gone," Lasorda said. "Mr. O'Malley asked me how I could do that. I told him I'd leave instructions to have the Dodgers' home schedule printed on the back of my tombstone every year. That way, when people came to the cemetery to see their loved ones, they could say, 'Let's go over and see Tommy Lasorda's grave and find out if the Dodgers are in town.'"

The thought didn't escape the older O'Malley. Before O'Malley left for his third year as manager of the Ogden Dodgers, he presented Lasorda with a marble tombstone, inscribed the way he had once told his wife he wanted:

"Here lies Tommy Lasorda. Dodger Stadium was his address, but every ballpark was his home."

There was one thing more added—a heart bleeding a single drop of blue blood.

After winning the pennant his first two years, Lasorda did bleed a little in 1979. Injuries decimated his squad and he finished with a 79–83 record. They bounced back in 1980 coming in second with a 92–71 mark, only to lose to Houston in a one-game playoff when both teams tied for first. Before the 1981 season began, he signed his fifth one-year pact with the Dodgers to dispel rumors that he might go to the Chicago White Sox.

"I don't know who was doing the talking about Chicago," he snapped. "I don't know anything about it. I've been with the Dodgers for 31 years, lived in this organization and want to die in this organization. I got a multi-month contract that was good enough for me. This way, I get a chance to come to a press conference once a year and eat."

With all his guile and all his wit, Lasorda is one smart manager. He did his greatest job of managing in 1981, leading the Dodgers from near-extinction in the championship playoffs and finally in the World Series, outsmarting Yankee manager Bob Lemon. It didn't take the Dodgers long afterward to sign Lasorda to his sixth one-year contract.

There'll be more hugs and kisses from Tom Lasorda while Frank Sinatra sings "My Way." The Big Dodger in the Sky would like that. . . .

FERNANDO VALENZUELA

He was special. But just how special nobody could assess accurately at the time. They watched him closely. The more they did, the more they liked what they saw. There was a mild case of euphoria in Dodgertown in the spring of 1981. After all, Lasorda has been around too long to get wildly intoxicated by spring phenomena. Yet, this rookie was different from all the others. He could throw a baseball with more poise than any 20-year-old who ever played the game. Coaches made comparisons before the 1981 season ever began about another Dodger lefty, Sandy Koufax, who had electrified the spring air 25 years before. It was only that Fernando Valenzuela appeared more of a natural. He could throw a ball with seemingly effortless ease.

The Dodgers got their first look at Valenzuela in the twilight of the 1980 season. Desperate for pitching help for the pennant run in the Western Division, Valenzuela left the San Antonio Dodgers and headed for Los Angeles. Although he spoke little English, he was unaffected by the call up, looking upon the trip as another stop on his baseball journey. He arrived with awesome credentials for a 19-year-old. He was unbeaten in his last

eight games in San Antonio, winning seven times, posting an enviable 0.87 ERA while striking out 78 batters in 62 innings! Of such performances are legends born. Still, that was the minors. The major leagues were something else again. It was a long way from Class A.

Valenzuela merely changed cities and uniforms, but the batters appeared the same. Five days after joining the Dodgers, Valenzuela went to work. Dodger historians will record the day as September 15. By the time the season ended, Valenzuela, the miracleworker, had appeared in ten games, worked 18 innings in relief, allowed only two runs and eight hits while striking out 16. He won two games and was credited with a save. Without his timely contributions, the Dodgers might not have stretched their hopes an extra day with a one-game playoff against Houston, which they lost. Yet, if he had been brought up sooner, there may never have been a need for a playoff.

"They told me not to be afraid to use him in any situation," said Lasorda. "Usually, you use a kid like that in games that are already won or lost. But we used him in tight games in the middle of the pennant race."

A interpreter assists Fernando in a post game interview.

He was something special, all right. By the time the season ended, a legion of Valenzuela followers began to form. The Mexican community that lives only a fastball away from Dodger Stadium, had someone to cheer for. There was excitement in the barrios and the word began to spread to southern California and into Mexico. The legend was beginning. Yet, it couldn't really blossom until spring and another baseball season.

Before 1981 began, the Dodgers looked upon Valenzuela as a starter. They were one pitcher short in the starting rotation, with Jerry Reuss, Burt Hooton and Bob Welch as the top three. In Valenzuela, Los Angeles had a fourth who would provide them with perhaps the best starting staff in the majors. Quietly, the Dodger management must have realized it long before the season started. In a rare occurrence, Valenzuela appeared on the

back cover of the Dodgers' 1981 Media Guide. Rookies are never accorded such praise.

Management's vision wasn't blurred. Reuss wasn't quite ready for the opening game assignment and neither was Hooton. Since Valenzuela had looked sharp all spring, Lasorda decided to bypass Welch and Dave Goltz, who was only 7–11 the year before and open with the rookie. The way Valenzuela had handled Houston the three times he faced them in the final weeks of the 1980 season was not lost in Lasorda's memory.

The starting debut of Valenzuela created an infectious swarm at Dodger Stadium. Although the April 9 opener was a day game, 50,511 fans turned out. In reality, it was the beginning of a new cult called Fernandomania. Unaffected by the mushrooming attention, Valenzuela took his normal cuts in the batting cage and, while it was still early, re-

20

The popular Valenzuela is mobbed by autograph seekers.

turned to the clubhouse. Finding the training table empty, he stretched out and calmly went to sleep. By the time the freeways began to bulge with the glut of traffic, the Astros might have wished that the kid pitcher had remained asleep. Valenzuela continued where he left off. He shut out Houston on five hits, 2–0. It was only the beginning.

Five days later Valenzuela faced the Giants in San Francisco. It wasn't exactly Fernando's weather. He is accustomed to the hot and humid weather of Mexico, not the cold and wind he pitched through that night. Still he struck out 10 and allowed only four hits in the Dodgers' easy 7–1 triumph. The run that the Giants managed to score occurred in the eighth inning and was the first earned one he allowed in 34⅓ major league innings.

Four days later Valenzuela was back on the mound, this time in San Diego. It was more of

the same. He blanked the Padres on five hits, 2–0, striking out ten in the process. Then it was the Astros' turn to get a second shot at Valenzuela. It was practically a carbon copy of the first time. Valenzuela again shut out Houston and, although he yielded seven hits, he fanned eleven batters.

In his first four appearances of the 1981 season, Valenzuela had tilted the baseball world. He threw three shutouts and gave up only one run in the other. His scoreless inning streak reached 19⅓ innings, and the Mexican population of Los Angeles was crying out for their new hero. The Dodgers' public relations department decided that it was, indeed, propitious to bring him to the people.

The first thing the Dodgers did was to feature Valenzuela at a free baseball clinic. Word spread like a prairie fire throughout the barrios of Terrace City Park, in the center of East

Los Angeles. The neighborhood is Mexican-American, many of whom only have a working man's knowledge of English. More than 750,000 live in the area which is referred to as East Los. Normally, at clinics like these, a few hundred youngsters show up with their parents. But when Valenzuela appeared, more than 3,000 Fernandomaniacs flocked to the field. A large group of police officers did all they could to escort him safely through the crowd.

That was before the clinic began. Afterwards, it was another story. Valenzuela did all he could to remain safe from the emotion of the crowd. He finally had to take refuge in the park's ladies room and was rescued by the perplexed peace officers, while the crowd chanted "Fernando, Fernando," again and again. Fernando-madness was here to stay.

In his next start, Valenzuela faced the Giants for the second time. San Francisco manager Frank Robinson hadn't been that impressed with Valenzuela the first time he saw him. Valenzuela had to convince him. The game on the night of April 27 was the first one in Dodger Stadium for Valenzuela since his opening game shutout against the Astros. Dodger fans realized it, too. The contest had been sold out for almost a week. Valenzuela showed Robinson the same thing he had when he first pitched against the Giants. He blanked them again, 5–0, striking out seven more hitters, for his fifth straight win. In the last 28⅓ innings, Valenzuela had not allowed a run. His earned run average was a microscopic 0.20.

The Valenzuela charisma was even taking over during the moments of a game. In his first time at bat, Valenzuela cracked a single. As he was standing on first base, the crowd rose and gave him an ovation. Valenzuela didn't understand. First base coach Manny Mota, who speaks Spanish, called time and explained to Valenzuela that he should tip his hat to recognize the fans' adulation. He did and the crowd roared in unison.

In the bottom of the seventh inning, Valenzuela was due to bat for the fourth time. Even though he was a good-hitting pitcher, Lasorda looked down his bench and told Reggie Smith to bat for Valenzuela.

"Fernando's stiffening up," Lasorda said. "I

want you to go up and hit for him."

Smith shook his head and walked away. He knew what pinch-hitting for Valenzuela would mean.

"No way," yelled Smith. "I'm not getting myself killed."

Naturally, no one else in the Dodger dugout volunteered to bat. Then someone shouted, "Send Pepe up there. We'll sacrifice Frias."

Later, in the ninth inning, a beautiful young female admirer dashed onto the field, ran up to Valenzuela on the mound and planted a kiss on his cheek, much to the delight of the audience. Unruffled, Valenzuela struck out the final Giant batter to end the game.

"That was the fourth time in five games he's struck out the last batter," pointed out Davey Lopes. "He's a star now. He owns the city. We want to do everything we can to help him maintain that, because he's a super kid. He's doing things nobody's ever done before. He's entitled to everything he's getting."

Lasorda revealed after the game that he had

some uneasiness in the top of the seventh inning. Valenzuela had stepped off the pitcher's mound and signaled for Lasorda to come out to him.

"He was pointing to his hand, and my first thought was, 'Oh, no, not a blister,'" remarked Lasorda. "Then when I got out there he told me he had broken his chain he wears around his neck. I took it and then I said wait a minute. I'm not taking that. I gave it back to him and he put it in his pocket. It's just as good there as around his neck, as long as he's got it somewhere on him."

The Valenzuela Express kept rolling. In his next outing, he made Montreal his sixth victim, 6–1. It wasn't as easy as the others. After being lifted for a pinch hitter in the 10th, the Dodgers crashed through for five runs. Valenzuela pitched strongly. He didn't allow a ball to leave the infield until the seventh inning. When he gave up a run in the eighth, it was his first in 36 innings.

By now Valenzuela's fame was international. He had pitched and won in the Mexican leagues. Now he triumphed in Canada and his fame was spreading to South America. The Dodgers' next stop after Montreal was Philadelphia. Valenzuela wasn't scheduled to pitch during the three game series. Instead, he was to open the weekend series against the Mets in New York. He was the hottest topic in baseball. The demands on his time for interviews were overwhelming.

The rookie phenom was chauffeured to New York in a limousine for a specially arranged press conference on Thursday. By now, Spanish language radio stations from Venezuela carrying Dodger games had increased from 20 to 40 for the game against the Mets. Mexican radio broadcasts zoomed from three to 17. All week long the Mets had advertised Valenzuela's first New York appearance. They even set up two extra ticket booths near the subway exits on Roosevelt Avenue to accommodate the large turnout that was expected.

Still more press requests flooded in. When the Dodgers arrived in New York, Lasorda did something about it. Uncharacteristically, he kept the doors of the Dodger clubhouse closed to everyone except the players. He refused to

grant any more interviews in an effort to allow his prize rookie some time to relax. It worked. Valenzuela shut out the Mets, 1–0, striking out eleven for his seventh victory. The crowd of 39,848 might not have appeared big by Dodger standards, but up until Valenzuela came to town the Mets were averaging 11,358 a game. Valenzuela had singlehandedly sold around $300,000 worth of extra tickets for the Mets.

Valenzuela's streak continued after the Dodgers returned home. In a game that was sold out well in advance, he won his eighth game. In a tight battle, he defeated Montreal, 3–2, with the Dodgers scoring the winning run in the bottom of the ninth inning. Valenzuela had duplicated what Dave "Boo" Ferris had done as a rookie with the Boston Red Sox in 1945, winning his first eight starts in the major leagues. The difference was that Valenzuela set two continents in an uproar with his performances. However, four days later, Valenzuela's streak was abruptly ended. Philadelphia solved his delivery, pinning a 4–0 loss on the Dodger sensation. Valenzuela looked at the defeat stoically.

"I knew it had to end," he said. "I'm not sad. I knew it was going to happen sometime."

What happened next was unexpected: a baseball strike. Valenzuela didn't understand anything about such matters except that for a period of two months in the summer of 1981 he couldn't throw a baseball in earnest. Yet, his torrid beginning enabled the Dodgers to barely edge the Cincinnati Reds to win the first half of baseball's split season. In so doing, it guaranteed Los Angeles a spot in the extended playoff season. Valenzuela finished the split season with a 13–7 record and a 2.48 ERA. He led the National League in complete games, 11; shutouts, eight; innings pitched, 192⅓ and strikeouts, 180.

In the playoffs, the Dodgers depended on Valenzuela. He started four games and won three of them, the most memorable being the pennant clincher against the Expos on a wintry day in Montreal. He pitched superlatively in the 2–1 triumph. However, it was in the World Series that Valenzuela gave his gutsiest performance. The Dodgers had dropped the opening two games to the Yankees and all the pressure rested heavily on Valenzuela's arm. Although his performance was not vintage Valenzuela, he tenaciously hung on like a champion fighter to beat the Yanks, 5–4, throwing a tiring 145 pitches in the process. It was the lift the Dodgers needed as they swept the next three games and the world championship.

There wasn't a doubt that Valenzuela would be named National League Rookie of the Year. But the Cy Young Award was another thing. Valenzuela had strong opposition in Tom Seaver of Cincinnati and Steve Carlton of Philadelphia. When the final ballots were tabulated, Valenzuela edged Seaver by three votes. It was the ultimate ending to a storybook season. No other rookie in the game's history had ever won the prestigious award. The Dodgers celebrated the honor with a luncheon, gathering in an Italian restaurant, of all places, in Chinatown. Lasorda didn't mind in the least. He'd eat pasta in Peking.

Yet, it hadn't been all that easy and glorious for Valenzuela. It never is for anyone born in poverty in the barren Mexican countryside of Etchohuaquila. The dusty town of approximately 150 inhabitants is some 300 miles south of Tucson, Arizona. Valenzuela was the last child of a family of five sisters and six brothers. His parents lived in a five room house and farmed a parcel of land just big enough to raise enough corn, cartamo, garbanzo and other vegetables and fruit. It was a family farm. The children worked the crops and some of the boys toiled on the other nearby farms. It was a close-knit family that went to Catholic church every Sunday morning. Valenzuela remembers it as if it was yesterday.

"We were poor, yes, but we never lacked anything," said Valenzuela. "We alway had food and clothes. We lived in a large house that had five rooms. My sisters slept in one room and the boys in another, usually about four or five in one bed. All except me. I would always get up to sleep with my mother. I was afraid at night. I had bad dreams so I stayed close to her.

"I went to the fields when I was about eight years old, I never worked. I just watched and played. My brothers did all the working. I was always more interested in baseball. I dropped

27

out after my first year in high school to play baseball. I was 15. My teachers knew I was playing baseball. They would come to my parents' home and tell them that I had not gone to school that day."

Actually, two years earlier, when he was only 13, Valenzuela's older brother Rafael realized that Fernando had professional potential. Even at that young age Valenzuela could throw a baseball with incredible speed. In his first sandlot game, he pitched two innings, struck out two batters and allowed two hits. But he was taken out of the game and told he was too young.

Sandlot baseball along the back roads of Mexico is pretty tough. The players take the game seriously, because both teams are putting up their money and betting. They expect teammates to bear down. If someone fouls up, he is subject to some heated criticism. It was at that early age that Valenzuela learned how important it is to win. Despite playing against older kids, Valenzuela was never afraid. Besides, his brothers always attended his games and if anyone made it hard on Valenzuela, they would have to deal with his whole family.

At 15, he was good enough to make the all-star team in the area. That enabled him to play in the state capital at Hermosillo. He pitched in five games, four of them as a reliever, and produced a 3–1 record. Valenzuela was named the tournament's Most Valuable Player. Later he was picked on the state's all-star team and got a chance to play in the tournament that was conducted in La Paz, Baja California. However, he only pitched two innings because he was considered to be too young.

Shortly after he returned home, Valenzuela received an offer to play professional baseball with the Navojoa Mayos which was located 20 miles north of Etchohuaquila. The contract was for three months. Valenzuela would be paid a total of $250, or just about $83 a month. To a wide-eyed kid of 15, it was a good deal of money. Valenzuela didn't hesitate to accept the offer. Once he did, he was sent to the team's farm club in Tepic, which was located in the mountains about 70 miles north of Puerto Vallarta, a burgeoning resort city on Mexico's west coast.

"I remember waiting at the bus station with my father and mother," recalled Valenzuela. "It was sad because it was the first time I had left home. My mother cried and my father wanted to cry. My father told me only to behave myself and work hard."

It was a maturing experience for young Fernando. He had left the security of his family and was cast in with a group of older men. Some helped him. Others refused to have anything to do with him. Valenzuela was growing up faster than the average 15-year-old. He spent the winter season at Tepic. As summer approached, Valenzuela signed a contract with Puebla in the Mexican Central League. The parent club sent him to Guanajuato. He pitched strictly in relief and had a 6–9 record. However, the hard-throwing Valenzuela led the league in strikeouts, compiling 91 in 96 innings.

His next stop was San Luis de Rio Colorado. Geographically, Valenzuela was getting closer to the United States. San Luis was a border town on the Arizona-Mexico line. Valenzuela pitched well, turning in a 9–2 record. After the season, Valenzuela came back home. His eyes lit up when, at last, he was asked to work out with Navojoa, the largest city in the province. When he was a kid of ten he always dreamed about playing for them. Now he was 16, but his dream didn't materialize because the club officials felt that he was still too young to play in the strong Pacific Coast League

Youth continued to be his nemesis. He reported to Ocotlan where he was denied the opportunity to start. Working in relief, he finished 3–1. For the first time, Valenzuela's temper surfaced. He asked repeatedly about being given the chance to start. The coach insisted every time that Valenzuela was too young. He was frustrated.

"I thought I could pitch and play as a starter," complained Valenzuela. "It made me angry. I would talk to the coach, but he would say no. I knew that I could do it. I guess it was natural, what I was feeling."

It was indeed. Valenzuela had three strong pitches; a curveball, a fastball and a slider. He was like a race horse waiting to break out of the gate and run his race. He finally got the opportunity on the other side of Mexico. He

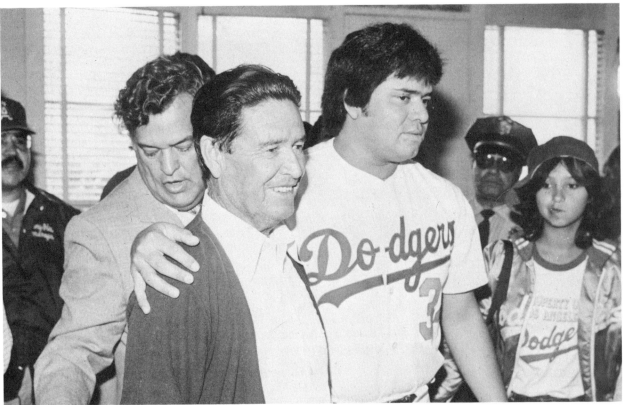

With his arm around his father, Avelino, Valenzuela hosts a Los Angeles city park baseball clinic.

signed a contract for $320 a month with Puebla of the Mexican League to pitch for Yucatan. It was all he needed.

"That summer I got my confidence, when the team gave me the opportunity to start games," Valenzuela says. "I always thought that I had the confidence and skills, but now I could use them."

In his very first season as a full-grown pitcher, Valenzuela won ten games and lost twelve. It was a decent record because Yucatan was a weak-hitting club. Yet, Valenzuela stood out. He struck out 152 hitters in 25 games, his high being 15 in one contest, and he was named Rookie of the Year.

Valenzuela was on his way. How the Dodgers found him before anyone else was like a scenario for a Mexican movie. Los Angeles' general manager Alex Campanis had several glowing reports about a shortstop in the Mexican League. Campanis dispatched one of his scouts, Mike Brito, to fly down to Mexico and take a look at him. Brito was a good choice. He was Cuban and spoke Spanish fluently. He also knew the Mexican

League, having played there as a major league catcher after being in the Washington Senators' farm system. He suffered a career-ending elbow injury in 1959 in a fierce home-plate collision, and bounced around the Mexican League for a few years.

Later, Brito settled in Los Angeles and drove a soda truck for Royal Crown Cola. But baseball still was in his blood, and he started an amateur baseball league to satisfy his interest. One year he recommended a pitcher, Bobby Castillo, to the Dodgers. Castillo had tried to make it as an infielder with the Kansas City Royals' organization but failed. The Dodgers liked Castillo's potential as a pitcher and rewarded Brito with a job as a full-time scout.

It wasn't long after his promotion that Brito went to Silao, Mexico to look over the shortstop, Lazaro Usganga. Brito will never forget the experience.

"It was Holy Week and both hotels were booked," Brito recalls. "I ended up sleeping in the bus station on the only four chairs in there."

The next afternoon, Brito was in the stands,

Valenzuela has often gone to bat effectively for the Dodgers

watching a game between Silao and Guanajuato. He began studying the shortstop very closely. Before the game was over, he'd come to the conclusion that Usganga didn't have a strong arm.

"I knew right away that I didn't like the shortstop," Brito says, "but I noticed that the pitcher for the other team was striking out a lot of guys. I saw that he always hit the corners and had good velocity. So, I moved right behind the plate; and Valenzuela knew I was there. He threw a three-quarter curve for me and an overhand curve. He struck out twelve batters that day. I couldn't believe he was 17 years old. I came looking for water and found oil."

Holy Week or not, Brito couldn't wait to telephone Campanis.

"Al was always bugging me," Brito added with a smile. "He would say, 'When are you going to come up with a Koufax?' And I would say, 'Just give me time.'"

Campanis asked about the shortstop and Brito told him to forget him. But he couldn't contain his enthusiasm for Valenzuela. Campanis wasn't sold. Brito then suggested that he come down and see for himself. Campanis did, the following year, and was convinced. He was ready to sign Valenzuela on the spot, but it wasn't that simple. Valenzuela was the property of Puebla in the Mexican League. The team was owned by Jaime Avella, who had quite a prosperous Volkswagen dealership in Mexico. He wasn't anxious to let Valenzuela go, figuring he would be worth more by the following year. He was right, too. By then the New York Yankees, among other teams, expressed interest in Valenzuela. The Dodgers were concerned. They had every right to be. They offered more.

The Dodgers spent some anxious moments. However, they were relieved when Avella decided to sell Valenzuela to them. It was a point of honor. Avella had told Campanis that if and when he decided to sell Valenzuela, they would have the first opportunity to buy him. On July 6, 1979, Valenzuela became Los Angeles' property. The Dodgers paid Puebla $120,000 and Valenzuela received $20,000 of it.

Brito was happy. "I'll tell you one thing," he said, "nobody taught Valenzuela." When I first saw him, the only thing he did wrong that I could see was that he didn't follow through like he should. I told him; and the next time I saw him, he was following through. That's the only thing I told him. The rest—he's a natural. I'd go to sleep in the jungle with snakes crawling all around me to find another Fernando. But, then, a player like Fernando comes along only once every 15 or so years."

For the final weeks of the 1979 season, the Dodgers sent Valenzuela to Lodi in the Class A California League. He pitched well, allowing only three earned runs in the 24 innings he worked. Yet, the Dodgers weren't quite satisfied. Campanis strongly contended that Valenzuela needed another pitch, preferably a screwball. He spoke to Castillo about it. Castillo had learned how to throw a screwball by observing Pittsburgh reliever Enrique Romo in the Mexican League. Campanis thought it would be a good idea to send Castillo with Valenzuela to the Arizona Instructional League that winter and teach him how to throw a screwball. Castillo agreed and had good results.

"Valenzuela picked it up right away," said Castillo. "You have to learn to throw it without putting a strain on your arm. I remember talking to Carl Hubbell during the Old-Timers' Game, and he said the secret is to throw it at two different speeds."

Valenzuela put his screwball to work in the Texas League when the 1980 season began. Before he was called up to Los Angeles that September, Ron Perranoski, the Dodgers' minor league pitching coach at the time, periodically checked on Valenzuela's progress.

"The first time he was getting away with some mistakes," recalled Perranoski. "The second time he was making fewer mistakes. The third time it was like watching a great horse in his last workout before the Kentucky Derby. When he first came to us, he was already a pitcher with excellent rotation on his curveball. He had a good-moving fastball but his velocity was below average. With the control he already had as a teenager, if he'd been real fast, I don't think he'd have ever thrown a screwball.

"You've got to have a certain kind of delivery. A screwball is thrown with an elongated arc, with great arm extension, almost over your head. Fernando does that. You also have to be real loose in all the joints, and he is. He was a screwball pitcher before he ever threw a screwball, if you know what I mean. He's super-smooth with super coordination. A screwball may hurt a man if he throws it awkwardly, if he needs a lot of elbow to throw it. The edge Valenzuela has is that he throws so effortlessly. He doesn't use the elbow at all. For him, that pitch is mostly just one big, smooth motion.

"Fernando will have to watch his weight but he isn't overweight. He looks the way he does because he's built the way he is. He's barrel-chested with a big waistline, but his stomach doesn't hang out. He isn't fat, not yet. The thing he'll have to learn pretty soon is that nice people are his worst enemies. Everyone wants to buy you food and drink."

Which is one reason why Brito serves in a fatherly role. He watches over his protege like a hawk. Since Valenzuela doesn't drive, Brito takes him anywhere he has to go, acting as an interpreter when necessary. He dines with him after games, making sure he eats the right foods before bidding him good night. When Valenzula's popularity boomed, Brito moved the young rookie into his own house.

Since he is so marketable, Valenzuela has engaged Antonio De Marco as his agent-manager. De Marco is a Los Angeles-based entertainment executive, who is extremely conscious of Valenzuela's image. Before the 1981 World Series ever started, De Marco had secured nearly a half-million dollars in commercial revenue for his client. His minimum fee for an appearance by Valenzuela is $10,000, which appears exorbitant. But De Marco has a good reason for it.

"To some people, $10,000 might seem high," explained De Marco, "but we felt it had to be high, to protect Fernando from doing too many things. I want people to say 'no' to $10,000. But if they say 'yes,' then it will cost them $10,000. We have turned down many offers: beers, brandy, tequila, cigars. It is perfectly legal in Mexico for Valenzuela to endorse those products. They say 'name the figure.' But we want to keep his endorsements high class, keep them wholesome, clean. We

want Fernando to be an inspiration for all children, American as well as Mexican."

In Mexico he is already a hero. Little children playing in the streets want to be like him. Instead of throwing a ball with their right hand, they switch to the left. His boyish innocence has touched young and old alike—in the United States as well as Mexico. He's the biggest thing in baseball since bubble gum cards.

"I just hope he gets his due," remarked Dusty Baker. "He's the one benefitting the least financially now. The only danger I see is in everybody trying to capitalize on him— baseball, the system, the news media. I'm not worried about expectations, because he's going to do what he's going to do. He's human."

Try telling that to millions of youngsters . . .

STEVE GARVEY

He's like something out of Madison Avenue. The good looks are there. That's only the beginning. He is also articulate, intelligent and mannerly. No one ever has to tell him he needs a haircut. He always appears well-groomed, even on the playing field. The hint of a whisker would be unthinkable on his strong, square-featured face. His looks are the mirror of his character. But the image has been shaped and commercialized by agents into one that has made him a hot property. He is only the tool. As such, Steve Garvey is perhaps the most misunderstood athlete who ever played baseball.

It hasn't been easy for Garvey. The word, 'image,' does not sit well with him. Actually, he is uncomfortable with it. It is strictly Madison Avenue sell. The hype is what bothers him. Garvey contends that he is the same person he was 15 years ago. He is, too. He is pleasant, courteous and caring. Somehow it all goes fuzzy in the creation of Steve Garvey, U.S.A. It has caused friction in the clubhouse and alienated some of his teammates, even to the point of fisticuffs a few seasons back.

True to his gentleman's role, Garvey refuses to discuss the altercation. It would serve no purpose. Besides, Don Sutton, the pitcher who came to blows with Garvey, isn't a Dodger any more. How Garvey has risen above the innuendoes and coolness of some of his teammates is a testament to his character. Most others would be affected by it. That's why Garvey is different, so special. Remarkably, he is not distracted by negative experiences. His detractors would separate Garvey, the player, with Garvey, the commodity. He is one and the same. Those with jaundiced eyes see him as two persons. Garvey feels it's wrong.

"If there is one thing that bothers me about all of that, it's that I sometimes think it overshadows what I've accomplished on the field," said Garvey. "Sometimes I feel those accomplishments have been restricted to the box-score, and that the writers have been interested only in writing about everything else. I don't feel underrated. No. But I do sometimes feel that I'm taken for granted. It doesn't bother me particularly; but in regard to what I've accomplished, it's sometimes difficult to understand. I am confident that as time goes by, people will realize that Steve Garvey is the same person today as when he started, and that he has made a contribution to his profession and to society."

Off the field, Garvey is idolized by an admiring public. Deservedly so. He'll sign autographs for hours at a time because he truly believes that it is expected of him. Envious observers consider it over-sell. They just don't know Garvey. He relates to autograph seekers, to the time when he was a youngster and did the same thing. It may sound corny today, but Garvey still holds to old fashioned values. Plain and simple, he's apple pie and ice cream. He is not affected by supercilious sneers, because that is the way he was raised. He would never think of compromising to appease others.

There can be no mistaking it for commercialism when it comes to helping others. Garvey totally engages himself in a number of charitable events designed to help others less fortunate. For openers, he has been a vice-president of 'No Greater Love,' a group organized to aid in the readjustment of veterans who participated in Vietnam; he has been sports chairman of a drive instituted to put nutritional foods in schools throughout the country; he sponsors a tennis tournament for multiple sclerosis and a golf event for an oral education foundation and has also gotten involved in several programs aiding child abuse charities. On countless other occasions he has visited hospital patients. Garvey still recalls a memorable visit he had with a youngster a decade ago.

"In 1971, I went to Orthopedic Hospital in Los Angeles to see a boy named Ricky Williams, who was suffering from cancer," related Garvey. "The boy had just had an operation to remove the lower part of a leg, and he was in a bad way. It gave me a hollow feeling, seeing him there on the bed. His mother said, 'Thank you for coming.' The doctors said he had an 18% chance of living. He was heavily sedated. I took his small hand in mine. His mother said, 'Ricky, Steve Garvey's here.'

"I felt a little squeeze from that ten year old's hand. He started opening his eyes. Although he couldn't talk, when he opened his eyes, it also opened mine. I could feel the strength in that little boy's hand. I knew then that Steve Garvey had a place. The following year in Dodger Stadium, Ricky Williams walked from the dugout to first base with Steve Garvey on an annual night for crippled

children. I don't really believe that I have special powers. But that night at the game Ricky gave me a medal with an inscription that said: 'To Steve Garvey. Thank you for giving me the will to live.'

"What I've tried to do is set an example. I've tried to demonstrate what a professional athlete can do for the public and with the public. I've tried to remain conscious of the professional athlete's image and the public's perception of it. I've always tried to remember that I'm representing myself, the Los Angeles Dodgers and professional baseball. You can't play before five million people a year and then just walk away. But, look, you're going to be categorized, no matter what. I'd rather have it that way than be known as an agitator, a troublemaker, a person who's hard to get along with."

The Dodger management wouldn't want Garvey any other way. Yet, to some of the players, he's a paradox. They can't fathom how he could spend so much time with autograph collectors, posing for pictures with children or just even talking and yet remain aloof in the clubhouse, expressing no emotion. Garvey is all business then. The horseplay and the joke-telling doesn't appeal to him. Instead, he occupies his time sorting his many letters, autographing photos or even studying a videotape of the previous day's game to analyze his batting stroke. In that respect, Garvey is the consummate professional.

"I've always been the kind of guy who keeps pretty much on an even plane," explained Garvey. "I don't get too low if we lose, and I don't get too excited if we win. After every game you've got to face yourself, to take stock of what you've done, to learn what you can from it. Sometimes there may be some resentment against guys who don't show a lot of emotion. They might say, 'Well, look at him. He sure is cold. He must not care.' They maybe don't stop to think that the guy is keeping his feelings inside because he does care.

"Sometimes, though, something happens that's so great, you just can't help but show it. Like the time Burt Hooton was going for his twelfth straight win against Houston near the end of the season. We were losing, 2–1, in the ninth; and Burt was sitting there hunched

over, you know. He'd tried so hard. Well, Willie Crawford walked, and then I came up and got two outside fastballs. The second one I hit over the fence in right-center. When I rounded third, I was just caught up in this truly great feeling. Burt wanted it so much, he'd worked so hard to get it; and I was able to get it for him. So when I rounded third, I guess, I must have kind of raised my fist. Then I took off my cap and waved it going into the dugout. I just felt so good."

Although he is a lifetime .300 hitter, Garvey had a poor start in the 1981 season. During the early part of May, he was batting only .225. Still, he was leading the club in runs batted in. One night in Philadelphia, he produced a seventh inning single that gave the Dodgers a 2–1 victory. Manager Tom Lasorda was letting Garvey play his way out of an unchar-acteristic slump.

There was some thought before the game that Lasorda would rest Garvey. That would have been like asking Lasorda to give up pasta. Going into the season, Garvey had played in 835 consecutive games, the longest of any active major leaguer. Although it isn't anywhere near the record of 2,130 established by Lou Gehrig, it is quite an accomplishment in the jet age of night baseball. Some figure-filbert reasoned that if Garvey played in every game for the next eight years, he will have played in 2,131 by the time he's 39. The baseball strike later in the 1981 season extended it another year to when Garvey would reach his 40th birthday.

Many felt that Garvey's streak came to an end in 1979. The Dodgers were playing Houston, and Garvey was holding a base run-

circumstances.

"We'd played a Sunday game and I started to get weak that evening," recalled Garvey. "I woke up Monday very dizzy, very weak, sweating. My wife looked at me and said, "You don't look good at all.' I got up, took a couple of steps and reached for the wall. She said, 'That's it. If you can't stand up on your own two feet, you're not making the trip.'

"I recuperated for two days. But we were fighting for the pennant and I flew to Cincinnati because we had a big series with the Reds. I played. We narrowly got beaten, but I got a couple of hits. My philosophy has always been to go out every day and play. I get myself into the best possible shape, and I'm fortunate to play a good position. It's an active position, but a good one.

"I simply feel this way: My first obligation is to my team, then the fans, then myself. If I felt I was hurting the team while not contributing, I would sit down. It would take a very serious injury. It's not just physical. It's spiritual, too. You depend upon a guy to be out there. I know how I've felt when we've had four and five guys out for one reason or another. I want to be dependable, to be counted on to be there every day. All I know is what I've achieved and how I've achieved it . . . how I've taken a 9–5 approach to the game. I'm not going to give them anything less than what the contract states. You get X number of dollars to play 162 games. If I were to break the National League record (Billy Williams' 1,117), I won't get paid extra for that. I've taken a lot of pain, given a lot of blood and made a lot of sacrifices. I felt I owed it to my employers."

He doesn't have to prove it to Lasorda. The Dodger manager has been a Garvey fan ever since he first managed him in Ogden back in 1968. Lasorda, with his fatherly image, is closer to Garvey than any of the other players. They have spent many hours unwinding together, either talking, eating or walking the streets after a night game. Lasorda can go to bed every night putting down Garvey's name first in the lineup.

"He comes to the ball park every day, ready to play," Lasorda says. "He's ready to give you his best, every day. He doesn't make trouble; he doesn't give anyone a headache; he just

ner on first. The Los Angeles pitcher, Bob Welch, tried to pick him off base. However, his throw landed flush on Garvey's jaw. Garvey was immediately taken out of the game and to a hospital where 22 stitches were needed to seal the gash. Since the Astros' hard-throwing right-hander. J.R. Richard, was pitching the next day, no one figured that Garvey would be in the lineup. Wrong. He was there, alright, and made his presence known with a homer, double and a single.

The last time Garvey missed a game was back on September 2, 1975. While the Dodgers were in San Francisco, Garvey was home in bed in the Los Angeles suburb of Calabasas. He was feverish and weak. Like everything else, Garvey remembers the

Garvey offers congratulations to pitcher Burt Hooton.

Garvey barrels into Chicago catcher Tim Blackwell.

does his job. I'll tell you, I love that guy. There's nobody I ever respected more as a person. You ever hear Garvey complain about anything? He has his share of problems like anybody, but he never complains."

Garvey did have his burden during the 1981 season. It was a deep, personal one. He was divorced from his wife, Cyndy, after a marriage of ten years. Somehow, he didn't let it affect his performance on the field. He never missed a game as his consecutive game streak swelled to 945. Had it not been for the strike-torn, aborted season, he would probably have

come close to 1,000 games. He shook his early season slump and batted .283. It was the first time in four years he failed to hit .300 or more. Prior to 1981, he had collected 200 or more hits in seven of the last eight seasons. The one time he missed was in 1977 when Lasorda asked Garvey to swing for more home runs. Garvey responded with a career high 33. He also gathered 192 hits and just missed batting .300, finishing at .297.

In the playoffs and World Series, Garvey was superb. He led with his bat and was instrumental in bringing the Dodgers back

from the brink of defeat. He batted .304 in the playoffs and .417 in the Series. It made up for the goals that he sets for himself every season, namely playing in every game, getting 200 hits, batting .300, driving across 100 runs and belting 25 to 30 home runs. There was no way of knowing whether he would have accomplished these goals if the season had been played in its entirety.

"What Tommy's done is to let me play every day," pointed out Garvey. "And the record speaks for itself. I'm the type of person who makes contact, even when I'm struggling. I imagine my everyday play to be a source of leadership. I play through adversity, through good times and bad times. It is a complex game. You want to keep it as simple as you can for yourself.

"I just try to keep an even keel. You don't want to complicate your problems by making minor adjustments. When things are going well, you don't want to complicate things by over-thinking. Just see the ball and relax. I've always said that if one person comes out to see me play, it's my obligation to go out there if I physically can. Even if I'm not 100 percent, I still feel I can do something offensively or defensively.

"I've only missed two of the last 1,000 or so games. I just feel I can pick a ball out of the dirt, or fight off a pitch for a single instead of a double, do something to help the team win. I always want to go out there. I always want to play. I'm a poor sitter. I did my watching in '71 and '72. The thing is, it's easy to sit out. Those times when you might wonder, can I really do the job, you push yourself. And you usually have a good day because you've forced the adrenalin to flow."

Garvey's insatiable zest for playing every day has given Lasorda some real nightmares. After all, Lasorda makes up the lineup card, and what if he decided during the dog days of August not necessarily to give Garvey a complete rest but only to use him in the last inning or so.

"I'd like to go back in a time machine," Lasorda says. "I'd like to see what Lou Gehrig's manager went through. I'd like to know what he did.

"One day during a doubleheader in the 1980 season, I decided to give Garvey a rest in the second game, using him only as a pinch-hitter to keep his streak alive. I didn't bring him in until the ninth. Then a terrible thought occurred to me. What if rain started falling in the sixth and the game was called off? The streak would have ended and it would have been my fault.

"Another thing crossed my mind. Say I didn't start Garvey in the second game and a brawl broke out on the mound. Steve would rush out there to separate the fighters. He could get his hand stepped on and not be able to come to bat. Peacemakers get hurt all the time. And what if an umpire clears our bench? Reggie Smith got into a beef with the third base ump one day. The ump came over to the dugout and threatened everyone. What if he had thrown our guys out, including Garvey, and I hadn't gotten Steve into the second game of a doubleheader?"

Lasorda's paranoia can seem endless at times. He began to worry about what Garvey may eat that could turn him ill when the team is playing on the road. The food found in a host team's clubhouse is not always what you would call gourmet. If anything, Lasorda knows more about food than any other manager around. Maybe he had reason to worry.

"They served us funny-looking chicken one time in San Diego," snapped Lasorda. "All I could see were the bones. I asked the guy, 'Did you make these chickens walk from Tijuana?' At least Garvey will never get sick in Pittsburgh. I told the clubhouse man there one day, 'You must have lost a relative in a supermarket. There's never any food in this place.' "

There is, however, a certain amount of danger during a game that Garvey has to contend with. There is always the trauma of a knockdown pitch . . . Garvey has escaped his share of them. Then there are hazards lurking on the base paths, sometimes created by design. After a game one night in Pittsburgh, Garvey charged that Pirate shortstop Tim Foli deliberately attempted to spike him on a play at first base. It enraged Garvey. Since he never complains, he was justified in speaking out. He had to go on record if for no other reason than just to make sure it would never happen again.

"I'd like to know who ordered it," fumed the usually soft-spoken Garvey. "That's a dangerous practice. Something like that could easily sever an Achilles and end a player's career. I don't like it one bit."

His annoyed reaction was so uncharacteristic of Garvey. He is a visibly quiet person. No one knows the aches and pains he has played with all these years—hamstring pulls, sore fingers, the swollen hand, the migraine headaches, etc. No one knows because Garvey doesn't allow himself to dwell on it and says even less. It's his way. He feels he is expected to play and just does it without any second thoughts. The challenge stimulates him.

It is amazing the strength Garvey draws from playing every day. It borders on being an obsession. He can make his way to Dodger Stadium, walk into the clubhouse and enter another world. He is, in a sense, an astronaut who has landed on the moon. There isn't anyone around more determined to play than he is. If he were a businessman, he would never be found taking a sick day. And if it isn't his style to back-slap and hand-shake, and he

seems distant, then maybe no one completely understands him. Some of baseball's greatest stars—Joe DiMaggio for one, Ted Williams, too—were emotionless on the surface. Yet they had their own individual sensitivities. All one has to do is recognize them and respect them. That's all Steve Garvey asks. And he really isn't expecting too much.

"My greatest single pet-peeve is people with ability who don't use it," observed Garvey. "I've seen guys with tremendous ability who waste it all. First, they're cheating themselves. Second, they're cheating the fans. I've talked to players about it. I tell them I wouldn't be talking to them unless I cared about them. I tell them that I'm talking to them now, rather than waiting until it's too late. I've done it with four or five people over the years and seen them come back, make strides."

Garvey himself had to make similar strides when he first came to the Dodgers in 1970. He wasn't an instant superstar. Far from it. In fact, the Dodgers sent him back to Spokane to finish out the season. He just wasn't quite ready. It wasn't his hitting that the Dodgers were concerned about but rather his fielding. It may seem strange since Garvey has earned a number of Golden Glove awards as the National League's top fielding first baseman.

However, the Dodgers first envisioned Garvey as being a third baseman. He had played that position his first two years in the minors, first at Ogden and then at Albuquerque. He not only had trouble picking up ground balls, but what he did with them afterward was another problem. Garvey has something of a 'scatter arm' from a dislocated shoulder he suffered in college. As a result, he wasn't consistently accurate in making throws to first base. One of the team's coaches, Monty Basgall, a former infielder during his playing days, worked with Garvey constantly. Long after everyone had finished practice at the club's training compound at Vero Beach, Florida, Basgall would drill one ground ball after the other at Garvey until he was too fatigued to continue.

"He's not afraid of anything physical, of pushing himself the limit," said Basgall.

Still, Garvey was a part-time player his first three full years with the Dodgers. His fielding didn't excite anyone, but his hitting had potential. Although he had a few mechanical adjustments to make, the Dodgers needed Garvey's bat in the lineup. After he batted .304 in 1973, they couldn't wait any longer for him to progress as a third baseman. Basgall's primary assignment the following spring was to transform Garvey into a first baseman. He appeared comfortable enough there his first season in 1974 and responded well with the bat, too, hitting .312.

Walter Alston, who managed the Dodgers in Garvey's early years with the club, recalled how hard the determined youngster tried to overcome his flaws before finally succeeding.

"He kept improving and there was no telling just how far his talent would go," said Alston. "When he first came up he was playing third and we worried about his arm. He did extra work on his throwing, and he looked like he had it under control. Then we began worrying about his hitting. Steve is so conscientious. But he couldn't hit the breaking pitch, and he couldn't do much if they jammed him inside. So that's the way they pitched him. He lunged at the ball terribly. Then he solved his problems. He learned to hit the low ball, the breaking pitch. Now he has the power to hit any pitch out of the park. He hits line drives. He keeps improving as a hitter, and now he's near the top. He's a fine first baseman, good on taking the throw; and he tags a runner on the inside as good as anybody I ever saw."

If anyone was born to be a Dodger, it was Garvey. He would not have wanted it any other way, either. As a youngster growing up in Tampa, Florida, Garvey was adopted by the Dodgers. His father, Joe, a bus driver for Greyhound, drove the team from one city to another when the Dodgers were in the Tampa area. Only eight years old at the time, Garvey took time out from school to make the trips while at the same time serving as the Dodgers' bat boy. Garvey retains precious memories of his childhood back then.

He was an only child. He remembers vividly the grapefruit trees that grew in his backyard. He remembers their exact number, too—eleven—because they provided him with his source of baseballs. In the spring, when the hard grapefruit had fallen to the ground,

Garvey would collect them. It wasn't long after that he would hit them into the air with a broomstick handle. He fantasized about being the whole Dodger lineup—Charlie Neal, Junior Gilliam, Duke Snider, Roy Campanella, Gil Hodges . . . He was particularly fond of Hodges. He was Garvey's idol.

"Gil Hodges was my hero, on and off the field," recalled Garvey. "He was a gentleman at all times. His handshake was something I still remember. I always admired the man. He always took time to play catch with me or say hello or something. He was not only a fine baseball player, but a fine man, too. I also remember Carl Furillo playing right field in Bradenton in water up to his ankles. He couldn't have enjoyed it; but he did it for the Dodgers.

"I was a bat boy for the Yankees and Tigers some, too; but a few of the players on the Yankees weren't quite what I expected. When you have an idol, you expect they're perfect. You hear them say a few cusswords, or see them refuse to sign a few autographs, and it takes some of the shine off."

It is no wonder, then, that Garvey has such a penchant for complying with autograph requests. Certainly there have to be times when he's too tired, physically and mentally, to perform the ritual as he does—often for an hour at a time. No one fails to realize that it is ingrained with Garvey. He sees it as a duty he must perform. The disillusionment of seeing some players refuse to sign a simple piece of paper for a fan, who's filled with excited anticipation, left an indelible mark on him as a child. He still is human enough to admit that there are moments when he wished he wouldn't have to accommodate autograph seekers.

"Someday, I'd like to go right home after a game, even if people are waiting for autographs, or let a big yelp of frustration out instead of holding it in," disclosed Garvey. "But I always like to behave as though some little boy or girl is following me around. Because, you know, if you do something wrong, damned if somebody isn't standing right there."

It's obvious that Garvey extends himself beyond the limits of the old adage, that all a player owes to his fans is a good performance between the white lines. It is also readily apparent that Garvey is a deep thinker and is well aware of life outside the baseball stadium.

"We are in the entertainment business," emphasized Garvey. "We are visible. We are setting an example for people, whether athletes like it or not. We do have personal lives. But as long as a player lives by the rules of society, that's what counts. Being an athlete, though, involves a strong mind as well as a strong body. That's what this country is all about. I believe the backbone of this country is sports. Where would we be without them? Perhaps 80 percent of our heroes come from sports.

"Sure, I wish there were more political, business and military heroes. It's true, we've got the DeBakeys in medicine and the astronauts. But sports have such tremendous impact. We are more approachable; people relate to us. Nobody can say that what I do is more important than cancer research or voyages into space, but it is more of a common denominator. I believe parents are the single most important source of inspiration and guidance. But we, the sport figures, are a secondary line as far as setting an example. It's said that 98 percent of the world is made up of followers and two percent, of leaders. I think that's very, very true.

"For awhile, there, when I was in college, you had demonstrations—anti-this and anti-that—and there weren't too many heroes around, people whom other people could look up to. But now, that's changed. It may be that the hero-type is appreciated again. Kids today might tend to admire a sports personality more than anybody in politics or public life. That kind of reinforces my idea that the opportunity for an athlete to go out and speak is something he should try living up to. He may, in the long run, make a bigger impression on kids than anyone else. I'm not talking about anybody patterning himself after some hero. Maybe just picking up something positive, one human being to another."

It is ironic that Garvey himself, perhaps subconsciously patterned himself after two other players. Both were first basemen and both, like Garvey, were noted for their clean-living, all-American image. Everyone knows about Gehrig's streak, one that seems impossible to surpass. But Hodges, too, played over a long period of time without missing a game while the Dodgers were still part of the Brooklyn real estate. Maybe it's more than ironic, at that. Garvey never knew Gehrig but read about him. To eclipse Gehrig's consecutive game streak of 2,130, Garvey would have to play through the 1989 season.

"When I think of what I've gone through just to get this far, then to imagine what Gehrig must have gone through," sighed Garvey. "Well, he was simply a phenomenal man. You could never measure it; but the Yankees benefitted psychologically from the fact that he was in the lineup every day, every week, every month, every year. He was the most consistent player in the history of the game.

"I don't think playing all day games was much of a factor then. I do think today's travel makes it tougher, though. The sudden time and weather changes—like going from a cold night game in San Francisco to a humid day game in Atlanta. That kind of travel pace causes things like colds, which bring weakness, which in turn brings on injuries. Really, Gehrig's streak seems out of reach for me."

Yet, it is not beyond Garvey to go after it. If the challenge is there, he probably will. Playing first base offers no great hazards. He is a contact hitter, which gives him an edge at the plate. Since he is so consistent in everything he does, he won't have to make any appreciable adjustments in his style. All he needs is continued health and freedom from injuries.

"It's in God's hands," Garvey says, smiling. "It's inconceivable the things that have happened in the past 25 years. It's a fairy tale for me—a youngster having his dreams and getting his chance to struggle and make them a reality. I remember how nice Gil Hodges was to me during those early times, how he played catch with me and talked with me. I remember and I try to do the same because I know the story has gone full cycle and that there are other little boys out there dreaming of playing the position Steve Garvey plays. It's what life in this country is all about."

It begins with Steve Garvey . . .

THE FAMILY

A cloud hung over Dodgertown when the team assembled for 1981 spring training. The success of two consecutive pennants in 1977 and 1978 had given way to apathy in '79 and '80. And rumors filtered out from the front office that there would be wholesale changes unless the Dodgers again recaptured the National League flag.

Davey Lopes, the erudite second baseman, knew the mood of the club's management long before spring training. At a team banquet on January 22, Lopes addressed the audience with an air of assurance.

"Because of your loyal support, we owe you a championship and this is the season we are going to give it to you," promised Lopes.

Lopes' confidence was refreshing. Although the Dodgers had lost their bid for a pennant in 1980 in a mere one-game playoff with Houston, a number of glaring questions about the team remained. The first was whether Lopes, at the age of 35, could bounce back with vigor after a docile year? Would surgery on Bill Russell's finger impair the control of his throws? Would there be more bullpen help for Steve Howe? Even more pressing was the question of whether Reggie Smith would rally after a serious shoulder operation. And finally, who would play centerfield?

Critics claimed that the entire infield was showing signs of wear. They began by listing Lopes, Russell, Cey and Garvey as vulnerable because all are over 30. By 1981 this remarkable bunch had played together as a unit for seven years—since 1973—a record for any infield. They had played as a group longer than Gil Hodges, Jackie Robinson, Pee Wee Reese and Billy Cox. In fact, going back to the turn of the century, they have outlasted the Chicago Cubs' infield of Frank Chance, John Evers, Joe Tinker and Henry Steinfelt, which held together from 1906 to 1910 and were immortalized in a poem by Franklin P. Adams. They had been an integral part of the Dodgers' success over those seven years, orchestrating Dodger pennants in 1974, '77 and '78. Could they endure another season together without allowing their effectiveness to depreciate?

In fact, this infield is something of a surgical wonder. Lopes and Russell, both outfielders in the minors, were converted to the infield before joining the Dodgers. Garvey played several seasons at third base for Los Angeles before he was switched to first. Cey, who played third base in the minor leagues and replaced

Ken Landreaux and ball arrive at home just about the same time.

Garvey when he moved to the other side of the diamond in 1973, is the only one still in his original position.

Lasorda was supportive of his infield despite uneasiness in some quarters. "They're out there playing because they are the four best we have," said Lasorda. "That's a simple answer. What's more, it's truth. If anybody could play better, they'd be out there."

Lasorda first saw Lopes in the spring of 1970 while he was managing the Dodgers' farm club in Spokane. Lopes had smashed a triple and went sliding into third base during an exhibition game.

"I saw him hit a ball in the gap; and I saw him take off, flying," recalls Lasorda. "I said, 'Oh, who is that guy?' Someone said, 'That's Davey Lopes,' and I said, 'Where did he play last year?' and I was told, 'Daytona Beach.' I

said, 'I'm taking him with me to Spokane.' "

Their relationship didn't exactly begin well. Lopes joined a team that was loaded with excellent prospects: Russell, Garvey, Bill Buckner, Von Joshua and Tom Paciorek. All eventually made it to the majors. Everyone but Garvey was an outfielder. One day Lasorda took Lopes out of the lineup, leaving him to sulk on the bench. In the eighth inning, when Lasorda told Lopes to go out and finish up, Lopes bolted from the bench and went into the clubhouse.

"I didn't want to be in Spokane," says Lopes. "I knew I wasn't going to be getting much playing time, not with the players they had there. Then one day, Billy Buckner got his jaw broken, and the next day he didn't even show up for batting practice. So Tommy put me in the starting lineup. Then about two minutes

Ron Cey

before game time, Buckner came running into the clubhouse saying, 'I want to play, I want to play,' so Tommy scratched me.

"It hurt me tremendously. It sort of proved to me that I didn't belong in Triple-A. And when Buckner got his four at-bats, Tommy told me to go in and pick him up. That's all I had to hear. My pride was hurt. I was on my way out. I would have been gone if Dick McLaughlin, who was a coach, hadn't talked me into going back on the field. I don't know what would have happened if I hadn't gone back. The Dodgers might have gotten rid of me. Tommy's word in the organization was like God's."

Unquestionably, Lasorda's judgments are well respected by the Dodger organization. At one meeting after the 1970 season when the front office executives were evaluating talent throughout the organization, it was concluded that the Dodgers were in desperate need of a second baseman. Lasorda spoke out and suggested Lopes. No one was excited about it.

Still, it didn't deter Lasorda. He was confident that Lopes could make the transition. He also wanted to make another change—one concerning Lopes' personality. Lasorda was determined to turn Lopes from an introvert into an extrovert, but when he talked to Lopes about both that spring, Lopes resisted.

"I felt they were just giving me the run-around," says Lopes. "I figured they were just shuffling me around the way they shuffled so many ballplayers before giving up on them. I thought I had come to the end of my career in the Dodger organization. I knew I was a good ballplayer, but I didn't think anyone else knew.

"Lasorda kept needling me. He kept saying, 'When are you going to start talking? When are you going to start making some noise?' He'd say, 'You have ability, you have a style, you have a gift; but you just can't become the kind of ballplayer you want to be if you're going to be introverted. You've got to be more cocky if you want to be noticed.' I could see my personality changing. Pretty soon, I knew, I really knew, I was going to make it in the major leagues, and I began to blossom. I began to get a little cocky."

"I tried to get him to be more aggressive," says Lasorda. "I would have to say it's one of the most successful jobs I've ever done. When I first had him, he never said a word. Took him out to eat in a place called the Park Inn. For pizza! With a priest who is now the ticket manager for the Padres! Sat there for two hours pumping him. Where you from? What do you do? Nothing! Finally, I told him I was going to make him mean and tough." Lopes became the sparkplug of the infield and was even the team's captain for a number of years. Lasorda is the first to point this out.

"Davey is like the guy on the basketball team who brings the ball down court, who sets up the plays. He gets the ball down, and then he gives it to the big guy to stuff in. That's what Davey does for us. He gets on first base, then he steals second; then Russell gets him over to third and the big guys drive him in. He's got to get on base to make our offense go. He's the key."

Although he never stole as many bases as Maury Wills, Lopes has distinguished himself

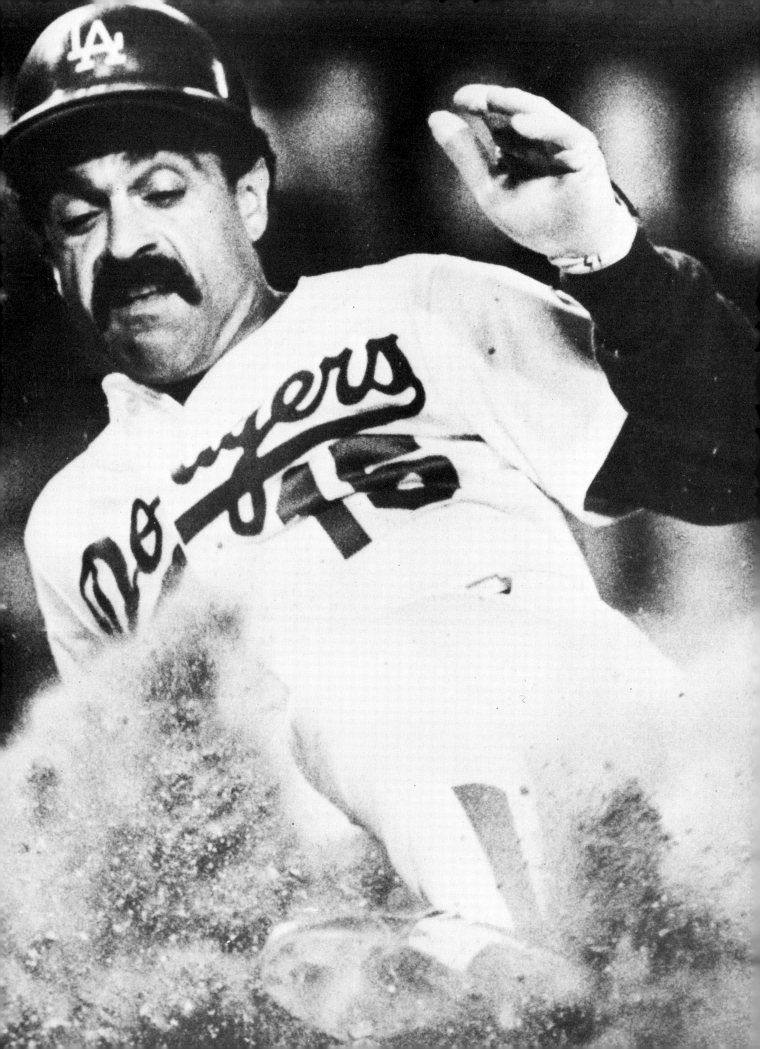

as a base stealer. During the 1975 season he stole 38 consecutive bases without getting caught, setting a new major league record. His career stolen base percentage of .831 is the highest in baseball history. He led the league twice in stolen bases with 77 in 1974 and 63 the following year.

The highest Lopes ever batted was .283 in 1977. Yet, it was in 1979 that Lopes delivered the long ball. He hit 28 home runs and drove in 73 runs from his leadoff spot. When his batting average slipped to .251 and the total of his stolen bases dwindled to 23 in 1980, Lopes came under scrutiny for the 1981 season.

"I think there are some people who might like to see some new faces in this clubhouse," says Lopes. "But I have a tremendous amount of respect for the other guys because they're good. Good players and good people. And when anybody says something negative about one of us, the other guys jump on his back. A lot of people don't think we do that, but we do.

"The fans, the media guys, they hear something second-hand and [they] pre-judge. And then there's the anonymous guy who doesn't have enough guts to use his name. That causes me a lot of problems. We've got different personalities; we come from different ethnic backgrounds. We don't live near each other. But the bottom line is, we have a lot of respect for each other."

While Lopes came out of a ghetto in East Providence, Rhode Island, Russell was raised on the plains of Kansas and now spends his winters in Broken Arrow, Oklahoma. They are an interesting contrast. Lopes is darkly handsome with a mustache and a mixture of Black, Portuguese and Irish blood lines. Russell is the fair haired blond with blue eyes and a soft voice. Lasorda managed him his first year in the minors at Ogden, Utah in 1966.

"Bill Russell looked like a kid away from home for the first time," says Lasorda. "So innocent looking, so quiet. Scared to open his mouth. He and the curveball were complete strangers. He thought a curve was something you went around in a car. He was making $400 a month then. Recently the bank returned one of his checks. Marked it, 'Insufficient funds . . . not yours . . . ours!' "

Lasorda's camaraderie with his players is re-

freshing. No other manager has quite the rapport with a team that he has. Of course, he managed most of the players in the minors. However, Lasorda is warm and outgoing enough to maintain these relationships years later. The players have come to accept his story-telling, and sometimes talk about *his* exploits.

"Did he tell you I thought a curve was something you drove around?" asks Russell, knowing the story had been told many times before. "Did he also tell you that we needed a police escort out of every town? He'd start fights in every town.

"I remember the first time I met him. He seemed like a drill sergeant. I was an outfielder then, and he divided us into groups. Then he talked to each group. I'd never heard anybody cuss and scream that way. I called my mother and said, 'Get me out of here . . . this guy's nuts.' He scared me to death. Most of us were 17. He was like our father. We went to him with our problems. Now, we're more grown up, and he's kind of mellowed."

Like Lopes, Russell doesn't hit for average. Russell's lifetime mark is .266. Coincidentally, he had his biggest season in 1978, as did Lopes, when he hit .286. Also like Lopes, his average began to slide after that. In 1979 he batted .271 and in 1980 he dropped to .264. The 1980 season was a strange one for Russell. He started the year with a foot injury and ended it with a broken finger. But in between the mishaps it appeared he would have his best season ever. He batted .371 in May, lifting his average to .291, and was voted the starting shortstop in the All-Star Game.

It was in a game against Atlanta on August 7 that Russell injured his right wrist when he slipped to the ground after rounding second base. When he returned to the lineup after a few days' rest, his hitting had slipped. Then on September 12 Russell's index finger was shattered when it was hit by a pitch thrown by Mike LaCoss of the Cincinnati Reds. He underwent surgery two days later and had pins inserted in his finger to assist the healing. It wasn't until January 12, four months later, that the pins were removed. Russell, who was 33 years old, didn't have much time to get ready for spring training, and there was great

Fernando Valenzuela

concern over his damaged finger.

While Lopes has managed to assert himself over the years, Russell has remained the quiet one. Even so, his temper got the best of him one day against the Philadelphia Phillies during the 1980 season. He got into an altercation with Tug McGraw and was ejected from the game for the first time in his career—not in keeping with his image in a baby shampoo commercial he did the year before. Russell smiles about it. He's well aware of where it's all at for him, as a personality and a player.

"I figured it's my first and last commercial," says Russell. "I enjoyed doing it though. I don't look for them. I'm not that type. I'd just as soon hide in the wings and do my job quietly. I'm not a flashy ballplayer.

"I've thought about how we don't know how much longer we'll all be together," he adds, changing the subject. "It's in the back of our minds. We've been denied a championship three times. The Dodgers are run like a business. You've got to produce or you're gone. We've been here together, more than eight years, because they've been satisfied with us. We feel for each other. Somebody criticizes one of us, we feel for the guy. And we don't want to believe some of the stuff that is written. We took somebody else's place. Somebody, some day is going to take our place."

At the start of 1981 spring training Cey, like Russell, was 33 years old. For eight years he had held third base, which had been the Dodgers' Achilles' heel for a number of years before he took over. In that time Cey had belted more home runs than Garvey and had played in almost as many games, but hardly anyone had noticed. Like the rest of the infield, Cey is pretty low key.

"I guess things just aren't the way they used to be," says Cey. "You have to have a big mouth or a special flair of some sort these days if you want recognition. That's not me."

In the opening month of the season in 1977, the pudgy Dodger slugger did what no other batter in baseball history, including Babe Ruth or Ted Williams, ever did. He set a major league record by batting in 29 runs. During that month, Cey belted nine home runs and batted .425. He got the Dodgers off to a flying start in Lasorda's first year as manager, and

Bob Castillo

Sports Illustrated had him projected for a cover. However, he was bumped and replaced by Kentucky Derby winner Seattle Slew. Then he was scheduled to appear on the front page of The Sporting News but was yanked once again for catcher Ted Simmons. A week later Cey's picture did appear in The Sporting News, but not as originally planned with "29" spelled out in baseballs in front of Cey kneeling. When the photo finally ran the baseballs

Steve Sax manages to get throw off.

59

Dusty Baker slides safely into home.

were cropped out. All that remained, appearing insignificant, was Cey kneeling.

"It was like they were saying what I'd done didn't count," said Cey. "No one in the history of baseball had ever accomplished that. Now if Reggie Jackson or Pete Rose had done what I did. . . ."

Actually, Cey has been overshadowed by a plethora of outstanding third basemen like Mike Schmidt, Bill Madlock, George Brett and Graig Nettles, who have had more exposure than he has. Each has been a batting champion or a home run king or, in the case of Nettles, a phenomenal fielder who has been compared to Brooks Robinson.

Yet, Cey is a model of consistency. Except in 1976, Cey has hit at least 20 homers and knocked in at least 75 runs every year since 1974. He has been steady in the field too. He tied a National League record in 1979 for the fewest errors in a season—nine—and set a club mark of .977, topping the .970 established by Billy Cox in 1952.

"I feel I'm as good at my position as anyone in the game, and I've got the figures to back it up," claims Cey. "A lot of them can hit better than me, or throw, run and field better; but I think I take care of my responsibilities for my ball club as well as any of the others. What your opinions are, are simply opinions. Base my career on facts rather than opinion and the things written in a critical vein don't work out too well. You play this game long enough, you separate yourself offensively and defensively. Otherwise you'll be thinking about your hitting when you're on the field and you'll be thinking about your fielding when you're at bat.

"There are a lot of egotistical people in baseball. I understand and totally accept and tolerate them. But that doesn't mean I have to like them. If I had it to do over again, and say I was the best, I couldn't. That's not me. It would be a waste of my time. I have never solicited publicty. In fact, I've turned some things down I didn't think were necessary. I am the way I am. I don't bother anybody and nobody bothers me. I have a job to do and I'm

Steve Howe

paid well to do it."

When he joined the Dodgers' minor league farm team, Tri-Cities in the Northwest League, there weren't many who felt Cey would ever make it to the majors. A Boston Red Sox scout looked him over and turned in a negative report. He appeared squatty at 5-10 and 185 pounds, the same size he was in ninth grade. Even Lasorda, who first got a look at him when he was a minor league instructor, wondered.

"I remember Cey, the way he walked," says Lasorda. "He really waddled. Like a penguin. There was no other word for him. I thought, 'Holy God, can this guy play?'"

Cey's performance in Spokane in 1971 made the Dodgers take a closer look. He batted .328, belted 32 home runs and led the Pacific Coast League with 123 runs batted in. He continued to hit during his final season in the minors with Albuquerque. Cey helped the Dukes and Lasorda to a pennant. He hit .329 with 23 homers and 103 runs knocked in. The next year he was a Dodger.

"An awful lot of people told me I'd never play in big leagues," Cey remembers. "But that just gave me an insatiable desire to make it. You can't say what a kid can do without knowing what's inside him. You can't say you have a scouting report that says Ron Cey can't hit or walk or talk good enough to make it without knowing what he's willing to give up.

"I was driven because I figured some other kid had played 500 more games than I had. Because of the weather and the lack of facilities and interest, we might play only ten games some summers in Tacoma. I was ready to run through a wall. Lasorda kept pushing us along by telling us that someday we were going to get our mail at Dodger Stadium. It was a real blowout when I did. Considering the obstacles, I feel very good about what I have accomplished."

Despite the consistency he displayed his first seven years with Los Angeles, there were some doubts raised about Cey the spring of 1981. In the previous season he had slumped to .254 at the plate. Only a strong finish that year gave him creditable statistics. In the final two months of 1980, Cey came on strong to help relieve an otherwise frustrating season. He

banged out 14 home runs and sent 36 runners across the plate. His most memorable homer came on the final day of the season, and forced the one-game playoff the following day against Houston.

Although Cey is not fast, he is quick. He doesn't like being known as "the Penguin," yet he takes the kidding that goes with it good naturedly. The players know just how far they can take the playful ribbing that goes on around the clubhouse.

Somewhat of a loner, Cey takes his baseball seriously. If he weren't such a streak hitter, he would hit for a higher percentage. Instead he slumps and then fights himself more. He led the Dodgers in walks in 1980 and his strikeout ratio, for a slugger, is low.

"To hit .300, you have to get a lot of leg hits," contends Cey. "I don't get any, so when my line drives don't fall, I'm in trouble."

Cey takes criticism and rises above it. That is part of his inner strength. Others may show anger or joy, but Cey handles the emotion without visible signs.

"That World Series game, the one where Billy Martin had a hard time, one writer criticized us all," snaps Cey. "I didn't have a single chance. I didn't have a ball hit within 15 feet of me. Yet the guy included me in his criticism. We've all been through it before, had our ups and downs. It's part of the growing process. We know what our strengths and weaknesses are.

"You have to play within your limits. The more you do, the more successful you'll be. We have a professional respect for each other. We all know what it takes to play the game for a long period of time. Socially, we don't do much together. Oh, we may have an occasional beer or two on the road. But Los Angeles is too big and we all live in different areas. What I admire is doing the job on the field, without your mouth. So anyone can talk to me about what I've done.

"We're probably getting along better now. We've weeded out all the bull that existed in the past. We've seen the business aspects of the game and understand them better. We laugh a little more and deal with our problems in a lighter vein. The thing is, we're not out there because of sentiment or nostalgia. We're out

Bill Russell avoids take-out slide.

Bob Welch

there because we're good ballplayers. The infield is the glue for this team."

That's the way Lasorda views it. Although youngsters like Steve Sax, Jack Perconte, Pepe Frias, Mickey Hatcher and Mike Marshall are crowding his veterans for a spot in the infield, Lasorda has confidence in the present group. He has a deep loyalto to all of them, including the formidable Garvey at first base. No other manager has the memories Lasorda has of his players, expecially his infielders.

"First time I saw Garvey," remembers Lasorda, "he's got on his Michigan State sweater with the rings around the sleeves, wearing a chain with a gold football dangling from it. Every hair in place. I met him in the Loehman Hotel, and he was exactly as he was today. I find out he's an only child. I say, 'No way.' He's not spoiled, got great manners—a respectful young man. And I knew right away, in Ogden, Utah, that he had political aspirations the way he started out kissing babies."

Garvey smiles at Lasorda. There wasn't any way a rookie could move him off first base in 1981. His talent hadn't diminished from one year to the next. Besides, he and Lasorda go way back, they've shared a lot of memories. Lasorda can't say enough about Garvey, and the first baseman looks kindly on Lasorda; he understands where he's coming from.

"I didn't bring my letterman's sweater to Ogden," says Garvey. "Tommy tells terrific stories. But I do remember the first time I met Tommy. I'd come in from Florida and walked into the hotel. I heard this gruff voice, telling a story and guys laughing. I heard him before I ever saw him. Somehow, that's typical of Tommy."

Jerry Reuss

Pedro Guerrero

In taking stock of his team in the spring of 1981 Lasorda had to look closely at his catching. Steve Yeager, the club's regular catcher for the past seven years, suffered a number of injuries in 1980 that limited his play. Although he never hit for a high average, Yeager was one of the better defensive catchers in the league. He possessed a strong, accurate arm. One year he threw out 34 of 86 base stealers. There isn't anyone around who is tougher.

Yeager earned the nickname "Raw Meat" in his very first exhibition game in 1973 after a bone-jarring home plate collision against Paul Blair of Baltimore. In 1977, he was leveled by Dave Parker of Pittsburgh in another collision at home plate. The year before, he was hit in the neck by a piece of Bill Russell's bat while waiting his turn to hit in the on-deck circle. He barely escaped serious injury as nine splinters were removed from his neck, some of them just missing a major artery, his windpipe, and an area that controls nerve muscles in the arm. Yeager was unflappable through it all.

What Yeager wanted was a chance to play

more. He realized he was selected to bat only against left-handed pitching, which reduced his playing time immensely.

"When you go with a platoon system, left-handers against right-handed pitching and righties against lefty pitching, you're going to have that," reasoned Yeager. "It's just that there are so many more righthanded starters in the National League. I can't be mad at anyone but myself. I should have been a lefty hitter, but I think everybody in the major leagues wants to play. That's the attitude you've got to have. A team can only field nine guys at a time, and there are going to be a bunch more sitting on the bench wanting to play."

Mike Scioscia was one of the most eager. He had youth on his side and he swung left-handed. That also gave him an edge over Joe Ferguson, the right-handed batter, who, at 34, was less likely to remain with the Dodgers through the 1981 season. When both Yeager and Ferguson suffered injuries during the 1980 campaign, Scioscia was called up from Albuquerque.

Scioscia, only 22 years of age, impressed the Dodgers in his brief trial. He displayed a strong arm and a good swing. Although he batted only .254 in 54 games, he made good contact at the plate. In 160 times at bat he struck out only nine times. The Dodger players called him Oral Roberts because of his healing effect on Yeager and Ferguson. His presence made the other two overcome their injuries quicker.

"People say I like him because he's Italian," exclaimed Lasorda. "They're wrong. I like him because I'm Italian."

Despite the fact that the Dodger infield had tinges of age, it could still perform efficiently. The condition of the outfield, however, was in question. The late season surgery on Reggie Smith's shoulder gave rise to certain misgivings. If Smith could not throw and swing a bat with the gusto that had established him as a premier player over the years, the Dodgers would be weakened both offensively and defensively.

Before the switch-hitting veteran was injured in a game against the Chicago Cubs on July 26 Smith was leading the league in batting with a .322 average. Only the day before that

Rick Monday gets home run greeting.

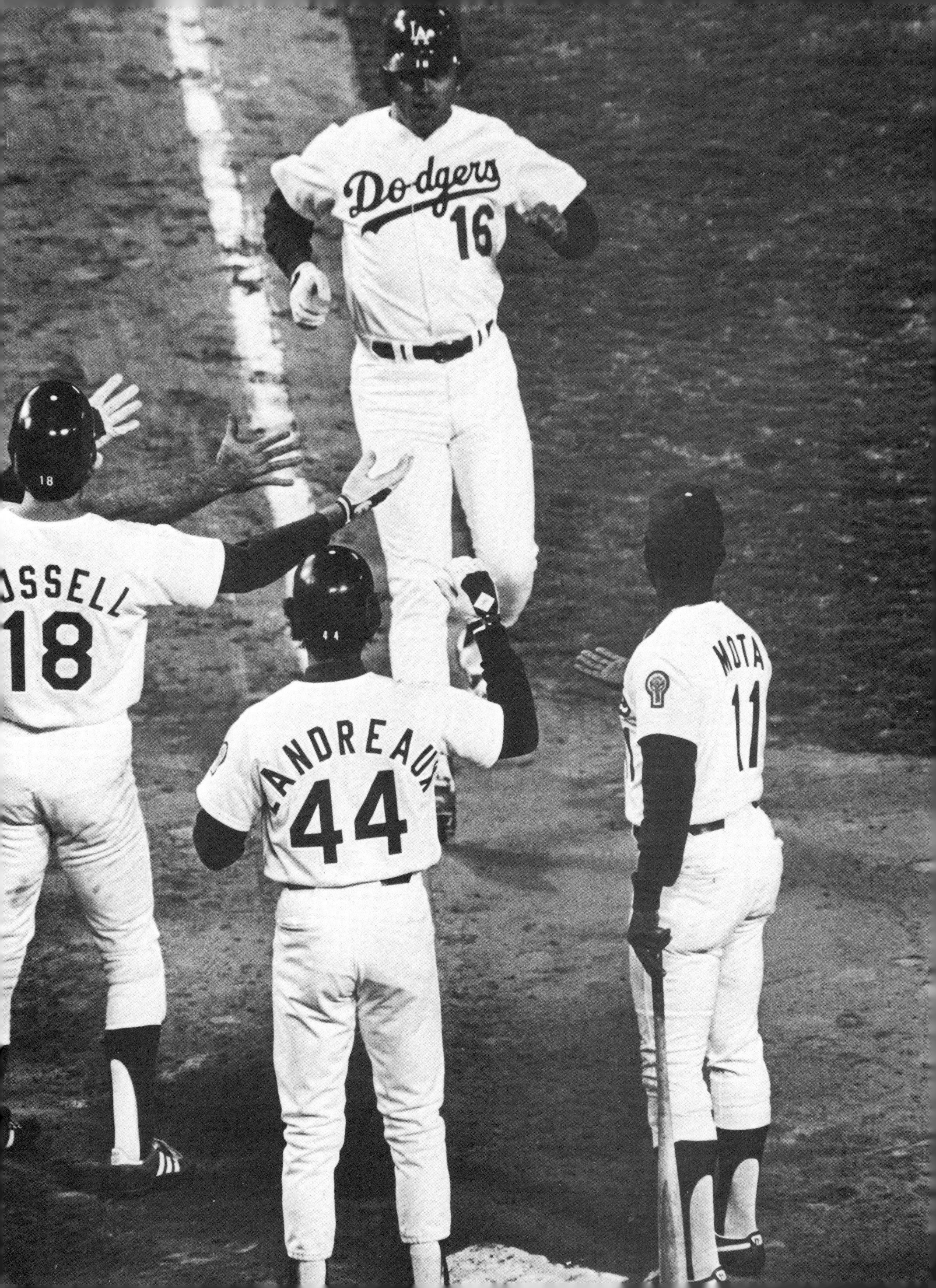

Dodgers
16
OSSELL
18
ANDREAU
44
MOTA
11

Reggie Smith lands on third base.

game, he had collected three hits to take over the lead, and seemed headed for the finest season of his 14-year career.

It was the second consecutive year that Smith was sidelined with injuries and, approaching age 36, he was potentially fragile. Injuries were nothing new to Smith. In his final year with the Boston Red Sox in 1973, Smith had a torn ligament in his left knee. It was hard for him to convince the team's physician of his ailment. The doctor claimed there was nothing wrong with Smith's knee that a cortisone injection and a few days rest on the bench wouldn't cure. Smith couldn't believe the doctor's diagnosis. Wisely, he sought another opinion at the Tufts New England Medical Center. There it was established that Smith did indeed have a ligament tear in his knee, a fact that was confirmed by a third medical review.

One day Boston manager Eddie Kasko walked over to Smith on the bench and asked him if he could pinch-hit during the game, if he needed him. The request angered Smith.

"I went out and got all my bats and dumped them at his feet," recalls Smith. "I said, 'If that's all I mean to you—a bat—then pick one.' Kasko called me into his office and asked me what was wrong. I told him my knee was killing me and that I wasn't about to jeopardize my future, my family's future, by playing when I was hurting that badly. He went along with me though it may have cost him his job."

Smith wasn't happy in Boston. He got off on the wrong foot with the Boston press during his rookie season in 1967 and seemed to pay for it the seven years he was there. The incident that first alienated the press occurred in Detroit.

"George Scott and I were rooming together

Steve Yeager

then, and our wake-up call was late," related Smith. "We were in a panic. We threw our clothes together and rushed out to the team bus. Well, it looked as if they were going to take off without us. That made me mad. I said out loud that that was a rotten thing to even think about. 'The bus always waits for the press,' I said. 'How come it can't wait for us?' One of the media guys said something and I got even madder. I said something I shouldn't have and sat down. That was the beginning of it for me. I was a brash rookie and they didn't like my comment at all.

"My relations with the press deteriorated rapidly after that. One of the reporters said to me, 'Son, I made you, now I'll break you.' I didn't help matters by sometimes not wanting to talk. It wasn't that I was mad at anyone. I just didn't feel like talking."

At the time, Boston wasn't the best place for a 22-year-old rookie to break in. Although the Red Sox won the pennant that year, clubhouse harmony wasn't an overriding factor. The players were then becoming a team of cliques.

"It was ridiculous," says Smith. "I sometimes wondered whether we were a ball club or a social club. I got along well with Carl Yastrzemski. Consequently, those who disliked him disliked me. There were three or four cliques. There was the Yaz group, the Ken Harrelson group, the Jim Lonborg group and later the Tony Conigliaro group, which was not only a group but a family. People would throw parties just so they could exclude the

Terry Forster

Jay Johnstone

guys they disliked. Then the other guys would throw their own parties and not invite the ones who hadn't invited them."

To make matters worse, the Boston fans became disenchanted with Smith, accusing him of faking the injury, and began to boo him. Then he earned the reputation of being a troublemaker when he knocked out pitcher Bill Lee with a single punch after being challenged by him following a game.

Smith carried a heavy rap over his head when he arrived in St. Louis for the 1974 season. He was erroneously depicted as a malingerer and an agitator. However, there was no denying the fact that he could play baseball. He was a dangerous switch-hitter and possessed one of the strongest arms in the game. Smith welcomed the change. He hit over .300 in his first two years with the Cardinals. Then he injured his shoulder on the second day of the 1976 season and his hitting fell off sharply. He was batting only .218 when he was traded to the Dodgers in June. Again an ugly cloud hung over Smith. A Cardinal had told the press that Smith was being sent to Los Angeles because he was faking a shoulder injury. Smith played in pain for the Dodgers for the remainder of the year. He hit well, batting .280. After the season ended, Dr. Frank Jobe operated on Smith's shoulder and removed a loose piece of cartilage.

Starting fresh in a new environment was all Smith really needed. He hit .300 every season for the Dodgers except in 1979 when he was bothered by injuries. Smith's impact on the club was apparent as the Dodgers won pennants in 1977 and 1978.

Although he admits that his reflexes have slowed to some degree, Smith can still swing a bat. He loves the challenge of a fast ball even at his advanced years. "There was a time when I could pull any fast ball," says Smith. "Now I have to look for one I can handle. As a result, I'm waiting longer and getting more walks. I'm much more selective."

The one outfielder the Dodgers could rely on consistently was Dusty Baker in leftfield. Approaching 32, Baker is in his prime years as a player. In 1980, Baker had the finest season of his five-year Dodger career. He batted .294 with 26 homers and 97 runs batted in. He also led the team with 17 game-winning hits. He hit more homers than anyone else in the club with his slugging percentage of .503, fifth highest in the National League. He accumulated only three errors all year. In the last two seasons, he had belted 52 home runs and knocked in 185 runs. Baker is probably the least recognized of all the Dodgers' stars but he's not the least bit upset by the lack of notoriety. Like Garvey, he dreamed about being a Dodger as a child. He was raised in California and grew up as a Dodger fan, his favorite player being Tommy Davis. In fact, he wears the same number, 12, that Davis wore, and doesn't mind assuming the role of the underdog.

"As a kid I always wanted to be the Indian, not the Cowboy," says Baker. "I even liked the lesser-hailed movie characters. The only one I feared was the Wolf Man. All you heard about was Dracula and Frankenstein, but the Wolf Man scared me to death. I mean he was fast. I was a smart kid. When the moon was full, I walked down the middle of the street where I knew the tree branches were too light to hold him. Walk on the sidewalk where they're heavier and that Wolf Man was liable to drop down right on top of you."

Baker got the nickname Dusty as a kid—and with good reason. He was always out playing in the dirt. His mother wisely made him take swimming lessons when he was only seven. Baker didn't object too much though because it can get pretty hot in Sacramento and Riverside.

A versatile athlete in high school, Baker starred in baseball, football, basketball and track. Yet, he was overlooked by the baseball scouts in the area. They didn't feel he was serious enough a baseball player because he would enter track meets the day of a game. Baker turned out to be a sleeper in the 1967 baseball draft. The Atlanta Braves selected him on the 26th round. The 18-year-old Baker signed for a $15,000 bonus and got in trouble with his father, who had wanted Baker to go to Santa Clara University.

"I was shooting craps with my life," explains Baker. "I don't think he spoke to me for two years after I signed."

Neither did many of the Braves when he

Mike Scioscia

joined them for his rookie season in 1972. That was before the colorful Ted Turner took over and the Braves were still a conservative organization. Baker's open style just didn't mix well and he recognized it.

"My music, my talk, my clothes weren't acceptable," says Baker. "I was arrogant. I was young. I liked to talk a lot and much of it was the wrong talk—both to the press and my teammates. We were losing, and I didn't like it. All I heard about was what I didn't do, not what I did do. Playing on a winning team is easy. It gets hard when you're losing. Everybody blames everybody else."

There was a players' strike that delayed the opening of the 1972 season and Baker learned an important lesson from it. "I thought I was the 25th man on the team," Baker tells us. "I didn't do anything during that strike. I didn't think I'd be playing when the strike was over. So the first game back Orlando Cepeda hurt his knee and they moved Hank Aaron to first and told me to get a glove. I was in total shock. I got a hit that game and then proceeded to go something like 0 for 20. I went right back to the bench. I know it was because I hadn't worked out. I thought I had blown my chance. It was Hank who told me to keep working. He would limp into the clubhouse like an old man and then go out and play like a kid. I worked. When I got back in the lineup, I was there to stay."

In that first season with the Braves Baker batted .321. He also displayed power with 17 homers and 76 runs knocked in. Baker didn't want to stay in Atlanta. He kept asking the Braves to trade him to California, and after he batted only .261 in 1975, they did. Baker couldn't believe he was sent to the Dodgers. It was the fulfillment of a dream. He couldn't wait for the 1976 campaign to start. However, in the off-season, he tore cartilage in his knee while playing with his dog. It cost him dearly. In his first year with the Dodgers Baker hit only .242. He had only four homers and drove in only 39 runs in 112 games. Dodgers fans voiced their disapproval.

"I was booed," said Baker. "People were leaving crank notes on my car windshield. They broke some lamps outside my house. It was the lowest point of my career. I had told

Derrel Thomas

the Braves to wait and see how good I was when I got home again. They must have been laughing out loud."

The laughter didn't last long. Baker had surgery on his knee that winter and was determined to make up for his bad start when the 1977 season came around. It was Lasorda's first year as manager, and he told Baker that Baker was his leftfielder. Baker responded by hitting .291 with 30 home runs and 86 runs batted in. The boos turned to cheers.

Like the rest of the Dodgers, Baker was looking for another pennant before the 1981 season and its threat of a strike.

"We got a great mix," says Baker, "the right balance between veterans and kids. It's the closest team I've ever been on. I feel I'm approaching my prime years. I've got that good

Manager Tom Lasorda

Mota convinced him that he should be patient and he would get a chance. When the opportunity came Guerrero made the most of it. Then, after being sidelined for a month with damaged ligaments in his knee, Guerrero returned to the lineup near the end of the season and finished with a .322 batting average. He had performed well defensively, demonstrating speed as well as a strong arm.

"I feel it's my job now," says Guerrero. "All I have to do is keep doing what I have been doing, hitting and playing good defense."

Actually, the Dodger outfield was in a state of mild confusion. With everybody running around nobody was really assured of a spot except Baker. There were still decisions to be made about Rick Monday, Jay Johnstone and Derrel Thomas. And there were other youngsters around, like Rudy Law, Ron Roenicke, Candy Maldonado, Mark Bradley and Bobby Mitchell. But none of these were considered ready for a permanent spot on the roster.

Even Monday wasn't certain. At spring training he had talked to Al Campanis about retiring. Campanis must have advised Monday to hang on and see what happened, because the veteran outfielder's career as a sportscaster was postponed for the time being.

All of America knew about Monday. He is baseball's answer to history's Barbara Fritchie. Several years ago, when he was playing centerfield for the Chicago Cubs (in Dodger Stadium, ironically), Monday became an instant hero when he recovered a burning American flag from two youths who had run onto the field behind him. That night, Monday was on television all over the United States. The next day, a photo of him preserving the Old Glory was on the frong pages of newspapers from coast to coast.

When the Dodgers acquired Monday from the Cubs in 1977, he was already 31 years old. However, he hit a career high of 32 homers and drove in 77 runs during the 1976 season. Although he's never come close to those figures in the four years since, Monday was a valuable reserve and a dependable pinch hitter. Besides, he is one of the two more jocular Dodgers. Along with Jay Johnstone, he's kept the team loose with his pranks.

In 1980, Monday began the season on the

feeling again."

The Dodgers had a good feeling about Pedro Guerrero. He had torn up the minors with his bat for five years. He made a couple of quick visits to the Dodgers at the end of the 1978 and 1979 seasons, and when 1980 came around, he was out of options. The Dodgers prudently kept him as a reserve and he was used primarily as a pinch hitter during the early part of the season.

He delivered too. By the end of June Guerrero was hitting an amazing .448. In July, when Lopes was injured, Guerrero took over at second base. When Lopes returned, Lasorda was intent on keeping Guerrero's hot bat in the lineup. He sent the anxious 24-year-old into the outfield—centerfield no less! It was a daring move by Lasorda since most, if not all, of Guerrero's minor league experience was in the infield.

Guerrero didn't care where he played. He just wanted to play somewhere. Coach Manny

76

bench, a spot he had grown accustomed to over the past several years. However, when the second half of the season began and those playing ahead of him had trouble hitting the curve ball, Monday was called up more frequently. Professional that he is, Monday responded. He batted .282 down the stretch and stroked nine home runs, finishing with an overall average of .268 and ten homers.

Overall, nobody on the Dodgers has been around as much as Johnstone. The 34-year-old, well-traveled outfielder played for six different major league clubs before joining the Dodgers as a free agent in 1980. The Dodgers signed Johnstone to strengthen their bench, which he did, batting .307 in 251 times at bat.

"I led the Dodgers in hitting last year," smiles Johnstone.

He also led them in laughs. He is the club's resident comedian. Nobody knows what kind of prank he'll pull next. Putting a pillow underneath his shirt and walking around the dugout imitating Lasorda, is one of his best.

Johnstone had good training for the role. When he first came up to the majors in 1966 with the California Angels, he roomed with Jim Piersall, who isn't your basic quiet major leaguer. The night Piersall read him the riot act was an experience Johnstone will never forget.

"I'm the captain of this room," declared Piersall. "When I go to bed, you go to bed. When I get up, you get up. When we watch TV, we watch what I want to watch. I don't smoke; so you don't smoke. I like chocolate ice cream; so you like chocolate ice cream. Remember, most balls are hit in front of you. Nobody ever hits one over your head, at least not the majority. So keep the play in front of you. I'm tired, good night."

When Johnstone saw Piersall on the Ed Sullivan Show one night he almost fell off the chair. Demonstrating a hook slide, Piersall slid into Sullivan and knocked him down halfway into the orchestra pit. There was no doubt that Johnstone was impressed by Piersall's intensity. He just couldn't match Piersall's fielding.

"But I was dedicated," explains Johnstone. "I felt I had to go four-for-four every night. Then I thought, 'Hey, this game is supposed to be fun. You can't spend 20 years burning

Al Campanis

incense.' "

By spring, 1981, Derrel Thomas was hoping he could land a permanent spot in the outfield. In the two years he'd been with the Dodgers the 30-year-old Thomas played every position except first base and pitcher in his role as a valuable utility player. In 1980, he played mostly centerfield and shortstop, filling in when Russell was injured in the final month of the season. His final batting average was .266.

The switch-hitting Thomas was signed by the Dodgers as a free agent after playing with San Diego and San Francisco. An enthusiastic performer, Thomas was a Dodger fan as a youngster growing up in Los Angeles, and is as aggressive as his idol, Maury Wills.

"I enjoy playing baseball," says Thomas. "Call it hot-dogging. Call it flashy, conceited, cocky. Call it whatever you want. We get paid to entertain people, and I try to entertain the

Bill Russell and Dusty Baker collide.

Bill Russell and Davey Lopes execute a double play.

best way I can."

As the Dodgers prepared for spring training, the best of Lasorda's pitching staff was Jerry Reuss. Lasorda had penciled him in as one of his starters along with Burt Hooton, Bob Welch, and, hopefully, the exciting rookie, Fernando Valenzuela. Lasorda planned on a strong four-man rotation with a fifth in reserve. On the basis of what Reuss did the year before, he was considered the number one hurler.

1980 was the best season of Reuss' ten-year career. He began in the bullpen where he was 3–0. By the middle of May, he had moved into the starting rotation and finished with an 18–6 record. He not only led the Dodgers in victories, but in innings pitched, 229⅓; complete games, 10; and shutouts, six. He had the most shutouts in the league, was fourth in wins and was third with his ERA of 2.52. He also pitched the only no-hitter in the majors and wound up second to Steve Carlton of Philadelphia in the Cy Young Award vote.

Before the 1980 season began, the Dodgers seemed strongly fortified with starting pitchers like Hooton, Welch, Dave Goltz, Rick Sutcliffe and Don Stanhouse, and although he preferred to start, Reuss had resigned himself to being a reliever. He had worked hard before training camp ever began. Following an off-field injury the atrophied muscles in the left side of his back had regenerated, thanks to a special exercise program worked out by Dr. Frank Jobe. Reuss also ran 30 to 45 minutes

Tom Niedenfuer

From left, Steve Yeager, Rick Monday, Jay Johnstone and Jerry Reuss record "We Are Champions."

every other day. And he worked on a Nautilus to keep his 6-6 frame at a tight 220 pounds.

"I spent most of spring training hanging around Sandy Koufax, just hoping to pick up something by osmosis," kids Reuss. "Actually, I've been relearning my pitching mechanics. For eight years I was a high-ball pitcher. I know now that location and movement are more important than velocity."

Reuss showed just how much more important on the night of June 27 in San Francisco when he spun his no-hitter. He would have had a perfect game except that Russell made a throwing error in the very first inning. Reuss'

sinking fast ball was working perfectly, and he threw only five breaking pitches the entire game. Afterwards, Reuss walked past the clubhouse where a group of newsmen were commending Yeager for calling such a smart game.

"It doesn't take a Rhodes Scholar to hold one finger down all night," chided Reuss.

Like Johnstone, Reuss has a marvelous sense of humor. On occasion they will collaborate. Once when Lasorda was doing a television interview, Reuss and Johnstone slipped under the sight of the camera lens and tied the manager's shoelaces together. Lasorda had all

Jay Johnstone, veteran prankster, is the victim of teammates' soapy hijinx.

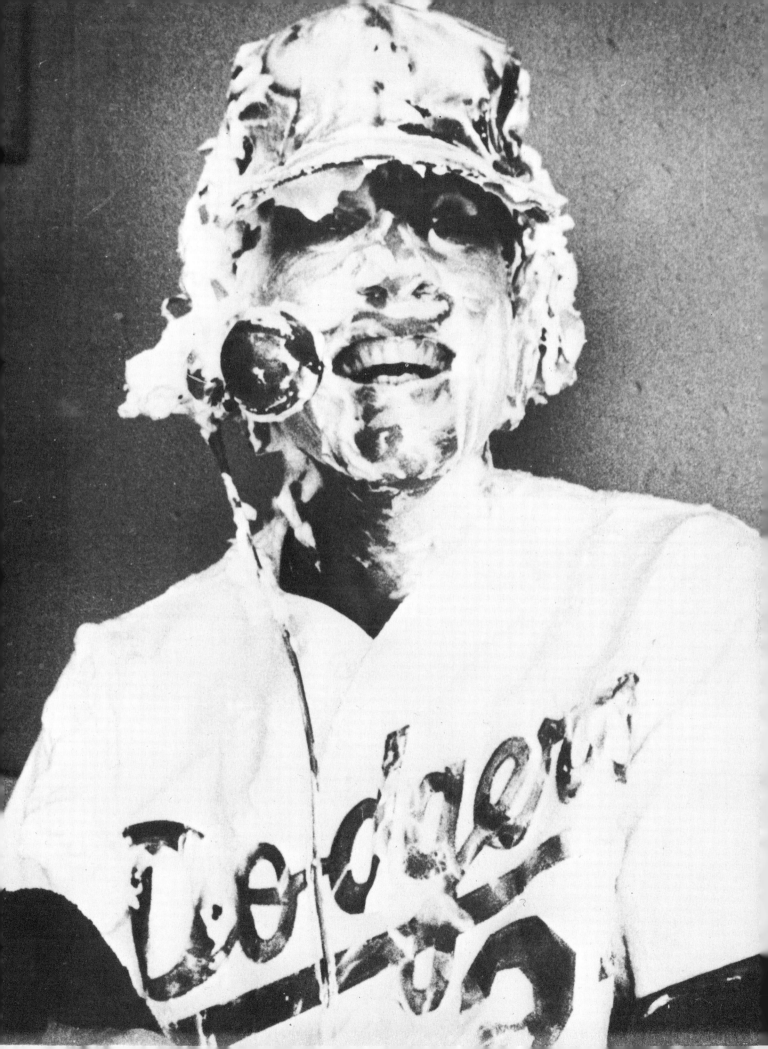

Part of a television sketch, from left, Jerry Reuss, Steve Yeager, Rick Monday and Jay Johnstone.

Steve Howe and his wife, Cindy.

he could do to keep from breaking up on camera.

"I want to use you more," says Reuss, mimicking Lasorda, "but my hands are tied. I'll tell you one thing, though, when I get the chance, you'll be the first one I go to."

Reuss pitched for St. Louis, Houston and Pittsburgh before the Dodgers secured him in a trade in 1979. Unhappy with the way the Pirates were using him, he asked to be traded. He was only 7–14 in his first year with Los Angeles, but after his 1980 performance, he was voted the National League's Comeback Player of the Year Award.

"There are certain things you can do to make sure you're traded," said Reuss. "You can put your uniform number on your license plate. You an buy a home in the city where you play. And you can become the player representative.

"I wanted to live in California long before I'd ever been there. I was the only kid in St. Louis in the 1960s who used surfer slang. The fellows in my neighborhood are as crazy as I am. We play trick-or-drink on Halloween."

It's not unusual if Burt Hooton doesn't laugh. He's called "Happy" by the players because of his solemn nature. Lasorda claims he gave Hooton the moniker because he once went to a New Year's Eve party and saw Hooton sitting alone in a corner with a deck of cards playing solitaire. Jim Murray, the witty Los Angeles columnist, claims Hooton acquired the name Happy because he smiled once . . . in 1978.

No matter. There is no denying that Hooton makes opposing batters unhappy with a frustrating knuckle curve ball. Although he suffered with bursitis in his shoulder in 1980, Hooton still managed to post a commendable 14–8 season. It marked the sixth consecutive season in which Hooton had produced ten or more victories. He has won 85 games for the Dodgers, more than anyone else on the staff.

Los Angeles acquired Hooton from the

Jay Johnstone

Chicago Cubs early in the 1975 season. It was one of the best deals the club has made in recent years. In order to get Hooton, the Dodgers gave up pitchers Geoff Zahn and Eddie Solomon. Hooton then went on to win 18 games that year, topping *that* performance with 19 victories in 1978, Hooton's best year as a Dodger.

As a youngster growing up in Texas, Hooton was quiet, just the way he is today. He was also one of the finest high school pitchers in the state his final year in high school. Cliff Gustafson, the baseball coach at the University of Texas who recruited him for the Longhorns, remembers Hooton.

"At that point, he was the best high school pitcher and the best high school prospect I'd ever seen. That's including Nolan Ryan, Ray Culp and a lot of others who went on to become major leaguers. However, during his senior year, he tore up his knee playing basketball and missed almost the entire baseball season. Had he not been hurt, he would never have gotten to college because someone would have signed him to a big bonus and he would have gone. As it was, when he came back late in his senior year, the scouts saw him pitch when he was out of shape and overweight.

"He was probably the most intimidating college pitcher I've ever seen. Teammates nicknamed him 'The Bear.' He prowled around the mound like a bear that owns the woods. I say this with no reservation; he was the best college pitcher I've ever seen."

With the Cubs in 1972, Hooton pitched a no-hitter against Philadelphia in his fourth major league start. Yet, it was against the Phillies, five years later, that he suffered a horrible experience in the championship playoffs. Upset by some calls made by home plate umpire Harry Wendelstedt in the second inning, he lost his composure, walked four batters in succession and was taken out of the game. There were many who felt that Hooton was rattled by the noisy crowd. Lasorda refutes it.

"He didn't pitch like that because of any crowd," Lasorda snapped. "He pitched like that because the umpire got to him. They missed some good pitches on him and he got mad. That's what happened there. It had nothing to do with the crowd."

Traumatic as it was, Hooton learned from the experience. "I think it helped me a whole lot," he says. "It was a very valuable lesson for me right then. I learned that if you do lose your composure and lose your cool, you're in trouble. You can't win unless you're relaxed. What happened then was not indicative of a good, professioanl baseball player. People tend to forget that five days later I beat the Yankees in New York, 6–1, and weathered that storm. It probably did a lot of good. You just can't lose your head like I did.

"Some people are cut out for national acclaim. I'm not. I just love the game, and I love making my living at it."

Bob Welch almost couldn't. At the age of 23, the hard-throwing righthander was 14–9. The season before he had been 5–6. Worst of all, he had fallen victim to an an alcohol problem.

However, Welch made such an amazing comeback that he was named to the All-Star team with a 9–3 record. His 14 wins, 213⅔ innings pitched and 141 strikeouts were all career highs for the determined Welch.

"I see a lot of Don Drysdale in Bob Welch," says Lasorda. "He's got similar mannerisms and that same look in his eyes. The only difference is, Welch comes over the top and Drysdale was a sidearmer."

The other starters Lasorda was hoping to draw from in 1981 were Dave Goltz, Rick Sutcliffe and Valenzuela. Goltz, who was signed as a free agent in 1980 after pitching seven years with Minnesota, was only 7–11 his first year with the Dodgers. Sutcliffe, who was the National League's Rookie of the Year in 1979, slumped 3–9 the next year. It looked more and more as if Valenzuela would make the starting rotation.

The Dodgers were also looking for help in the bullpen. Steve Howe, with only a half-year experience in professional baseball, turned out to be the Dodgers' stopper in 1980. Though he was 7–9, Howe led the club with 17 saves and was voted the National League's Rookie of the Year. He had a 94 MPH fastball and displayed good control for a rookie.

The only other veterans were Terry Forster, another lefty who was recovering from elbow trouble, and righthanders Bob Castillo and

Steve Howe and Dusty Baker share a laugh.

Don Stanhouse. Two rookies were being considered: Dave Stewart and Ted Power.

Then, in the most bizarre season ever seen in baseball, the Dodgers got off fast on the arm of Valenzuela, Los Angeles won ten of its first twelve games, and the legend of Valenzuela was born. He won four of the games, three of them shutouts. When May 23 dawned, the Dodgers had a breathless 29–11 record, and were 6½ games ahead of Cincinnati, who was panting in second place. The Dodgers were in first place simply because their pitching was unusually strong. Valenzuela led with an 8–2 record and a 1.24 ERA. Hooton was next with a 6–0 mark and a 2.11 ERA, followed by Reuss, who was 4–1 with a 1.50 ERA. The ERA of the entire staff was an exceptional 2.35.

The infield held together, although Lopes and Russell had trouble hitting. When Reggie Smith needed more time to overcome his shoulder injury the Dodgers acquired Ken Landreaux from Minnesota. Landreaux batted a solid .280 and had timely hits with runners on base to complement the hitting of Baker and Cey. Using Welch, the four-man pitching rotation worked well and the bullpen was fine. Baseball's second major strike, the first after a season had begun, interrupted the national pastime on June 12 as the Dodgers were ahead of Cincinnati by just a half-game margin. After the strike was settled two months later, Commissioner Bowie Kuhn decreed a split season. Since Los Angeles had won the first season, they were automatically eligible for the championship playoffs.

It was only the beginning of a blue heaven. . . .

HOUSTON PLAYOFF

The Dodger hitters were not excited about going to Houston and its oppressive bubble, the Astrodome. Outdoor-loving Californians, they were unhappy that the first two games of the divisional playoffs were to be played indoors, in what seemed like a vacuum. They all detested the artificial turf playing surface, and the team's power hitters were appalled by the long power alleys, which made hitting home runs almost impossible. What's more, the batters complained that the ball just doesn't carry in the Dome. Ask any Dodger; he'll say he'd prefer to play Cincinnati.

There were a few additional reasons for their reticence, namely Houston's starting pitchers. Nolan Ryan, who had hurled a no-hitter against the Dodgers just weeks before, and was scheduled to pitch the opener, had a 1.11 ERA in the Astrodome; Bob Knepper had a 1.22; and Joe Nieko, a 1.94. It seemed it would take a shutout by a Dodger pitcher just to remain tied.

The Dodgers' performance during the past month had been somewhat less than brilliant. On September 18 Los Angeles had been only two games behind division-leading Houston. They were hoping to overtake the Astros, turn back Cincinnati, and to capture both halves of baseball's divided season. Unfortunately, their skid began that night, in front of their home fans as they were closing out a victory over the Reds. Johnny Bench was sent up as a pinch-hitter in the ninth inning as there were two out and two runners on base. Bench didn't leave them there. He whacked a three-run homer to defeat the Dodgers 5–4. The Dodgers never quite recovered and went on to lose five games in a row, their longest streak in two years. Then there was Ryan's no-hitter, and the very next day ex-Dodger Don Sutton blanked them on two hits. That made two consecutive games in which Los Angeles had lost with just two hits. To make matters worse, the bullpen went almost three weeks, for a total of 13 appearances, before closing out a game without yielding a run, and the team's offense was generally docile.

"Everything turned around after that," says Lasorda. "I felt we could win the second half even after Ryan no-hit us. I felt we could get back into it. But we just weren't scoring any runs. And it was the failure of the offense along with the problems in the bullpen that cost us."

The Dodgers ineptitude may have been

Cesar Cedeno dives back to first base in opening game as Garvey takes catcher Mike Scioscia's throw.

Cedeno steals second base under Bill Russell's tag.

most obvious in the final laps of the season, but in reality, their trouble began earlier, long before Bench did his thing. On September 9, Cey was hit by a fastball thrown by Tom Griffin of San Francisco. Cey had thrown up his arm to protect his head from the missile and suffered a broken bone in his left forearm. With Cey sidelined, the Dodgers dropped eleven of their next 16 games. On September 28, when they were finally eliminated from the second-half chase, they had lost eight of their last ten games. Lasorda knew the reason.

"If you recall, the day Penguin got hurt I said that maybe now people will see just how valuable he's been to this club—his consistency, games played, runs batted in, home runs," pointed out Lasorda. "There's probably just one other third baseman who's been as productive as Cey the last several years, and that's the fellow at Philadelphia.

"We wanted to win the second half very badly, not merely because of the added home-field advantage, but also because of the pride involved. But we fell short. I'll say this though: not once did I hear anyone say, 'Hey, what the heck do we care? We've got a playoff spot.' We all wanted to win."

No one more than Cey. At the time of his injury he was leading the club in homers, with 13. He had the cast removed from his arm on September 30 and was informed that he could begin taking batting practice in a week. But he wouldn't be well enough to face the Astros at all. Guerrero probably missed him more than any other Dodger. When Cey got hurt, Guerrero was playing well in right field and hitting .316. For some reason, when he took over for Cey at third, his hitting was affected. He went through an eight for 45 skid and his average dropped to .298.

"Our offense would function better if we played Cincinnati rather than Houston," remarked Cey. "Houston has the best pitching in the league and much of our power is nullified when we play in the Astrodome. I'm through for the season unless we win our division. By the time I take batting practice, I'll have been out a month and I'll only have six days to get ready for the league playoffs. That may be too much to ask. Everything is out of my hands. No matter how much I do, it's up to the team and Mother Nature."

GAME ONE

The Dodgers didn't have to worry about Mother Nature in the Houston greenhouse. Ryan was their concern. Lasorda named Valenzuela to oppose him. It was the Dodgers' best against the Astros' ace. Both had had outstanding seasons. Valenzuela had shutout the Astros twice during the season, and he was the loser when Ryan hurled his no-hitter. It was a match-up of Cy Young Award candidates.

Valenzuela seemed unaffected by any opening game pressure. He frolicked in the outfield during the Dodgers' workout the day before the opener, imitating a soccer player. "Tight?" asked Lasorda. "Hah, that's the last thing I worry about with Fernando Valenzuela after what he's been through."

Scioscia concurred.

"He looks the same way he did before the opening game of the season when he threw 20 minutes of batting practice and they told him he was going to start the next day," said the catcher. "He'll be all right."

The one thing Valenzuela and Scioscia had

Tom Lasorda

Fernando Valenzuela

Fernando Valenzuela

Steve Garvey

Steve Garvey

Burt Hooton

Jerry Reuss

Steve Howe

Bob Welch

Ken Landreaux

Dusty Baker

Rick Monday

Pedro Guerrero

Davey Lopes

Ron Cey

Bill Russell

Davey Lopes couldn't quite reach Terry Puhl's short fly ball in sixth inning.

Game 1	1	2	3	4	5	6	7	8	9	Total
Los Angeles	0	0	0	0	0	0	1	0	0	1
Houston	0	0	0	0	0	1	0	0	2	3

to consider was the Astros' speed. Centerfielder Tony Scott, recently acquired from St. Louis, only provided Houston with additional speed. Phil Garner, the second baseman from Pittsburgh, made them more aggressive. "If they get the lead, they start running on you, hitting and running, doing all that crazy stuff," warned Baker. "They bring in four, five pitchers until they find the one who's throwing good that day."

Ryan started the game by getting Lopes on a grounder. Landreaux touched him for a single but any Dodger hopes for a score were dashed when Baker hit into a double play. Valenzuela didn't have any trouble his first

time on the mound, retiring the Astros in order, striking out Garner and Scott to end the inning.

After Monday drew a one-out walk, Ryan fanned Guerrero and Scioscia in the second inning. With one out, Cesar Cedeno got the first hit off Valenzuela when the Astros came up to bat. With two out, he stole second but Valenzuela got Kiko Garcia on a grounder, preventing any damage.

Both teams were retired in order over the next two innings. As in the last time they met, Valenzuela and Ryan were locked in another tight pitching duel. After the Dodgers were set down quietly for the third straight inning, the

Astros tried to get something going. When they came up in the fifth, with one out, Art Howe singled. However, he took too much liberty leading off first base and Valenzuela quickly picked him off.

Still, the Dodger bats were silent. Ryan, looking strong and sharp, put them away for the fourth consecutive inning. He struck out both Valenzuela and Lopes to end the frame. Ryan now was working on a string of 14 hitters who had failed to reach base. The crowd of 44,836 was enjoying it.

Valenzuela began the sixth routinely. He got Alan Ashby on a fly ball and Ryan on a grounder. Terry Puhl collected the third hit off Valenzuela, a single to right. Expecting the Houston lead-off hitter to steal, Valenzuela pitched out. He did it a second time, but Puhl didn't break for second. Behind 2–0, Garner worked Valenzuela for the first walk of the well-pitched game. It was the first time either team had two runners on base. Valenzuela bore down on Scott, working the count to 2–2. The irrepressible rookie then jammed Scott with a fastball on his hands. Scott swung and sent a lazy pop into short right center field. Monday and Landreaux raced in. Lopes glided out and appeared to have the ball in sight. He tried to overtake it and make an over-the-shoulder catch, but couldn't. The ball fell onto the Astro turf. Puhl scampered home with the game's first run. Garner sped to third and Scott wound up on second. Valenzuela closed out the inning by getting Jose Cruz on a ground ball.

Ryan started off the seventh stanza by whiffing Landreaux, his sixth strikeout of the game. Baker flied to Puhl for the second out. Ryan looked unhittable. Baker was the 16th straight batter he had retired. Garvey was next. Ryan tried a fastball. Garvey was ready for it. He drilled the pitch over the 400-foot marker in left center for a game-tying homer.

Leading off for Houston, Cedeno smashed a one-hop double past Guerrero. Monday then saved a run with a shoestring catch on Howe's bid for a base hit. After Garcia made the second out, Ashby was walked intentionally, and Cedeno got a big lead off second base and proceeded to steal third. Lopes squelched the threat with a neat backhand stop of Ryan's

bouncer, to force Ashby.

The Dodgers couldn't get anywhere against Ryan in the eighth. They went out in order. It was getting late. Valenzuela had to hang tough and match Ryan, especially after Puhl punched out a single to start the Astros off. Valenzuela answered back and retired the next three batters without any further trouble. The fans couldn't have ordered a tighter pitching contest. However, Valenzuela's part in the 1–1 struggle came to an end in the ninth. Johnstone batted for him and grounded out. Ryan closed the inning masterfully, making Lopes his seventh strike out victim and getting Landreaux on a grounder.

It was now up to Sammy Stewart to contain the Astros. He started out sharply by striking out Cedeno. Howe made the second out by lining to Landreaux. Craig Reynolds pinch-hit for Garcia, coming through with a single, which brought up Ashby, who had hit only four homers during the season and 30 in his eight-year career. Stewart challenged him with a fastball. Ashby swung and drove the ball down the right field line that carried into the seats for a dramatic game-winning home run, 3–1. Ashby jumped around the bases. Ryan had beaten the Dodgers again on a home run by an unlikely long ball hitter.

"A Walter Mitty dream," exclaimed a happy Ashby. "I was elated beyond words. That's why I was circling the bases with my arms above my head. You don't see a guy who hits four homers a year doing that. I can't describe the excitement I felt. I can't say I didn't think about a homer. It's a hard thing for a guy who's hit only four to say, but I was trying to get a good out—see if I could drive one. Most guys think that way—two out, bottom of the ninth, tie game."

If Lopes had caught Scott's pop, it would have been a different ending. Valenzuela would still have been working on a shutout. Lopes, somewhat subdued, explained why he missed the blooper that drove in the only run against Valenzuela.

"I knew it was trouble," he said. "I just ran back to where I thought it would land and when I got there I realized that was not where the ball was. It was a do-or-die play."

Baker came by and tried to offer some solace as Lopes was being questioned by newsmen.

"In defense of Davey . . ." began Baker.

Lopes didn't let him finish.

"I don't need any defense," he snapped.

What the Dodgers needed was some offense. . . .

GAME TWO

Houston had accomplished the first half of its mission, and Virdon arranged his pitching plans to make certain he had every edge. He decided to bypass Bob Knepper, who was due next in his rotation, and go with Joe Nierko. Although Knepper was 9–5 on the year compared to Nierko's 9–9 record, Virdon leaned toward the older righthander, recalling the final weekend series of the season when Knepper lasted only four innings against the Dodgers.

Knepper actually pitched better in the Astrodome than he did outdoors. He was 8–2 in Houston with a 1.22 ERA. On the road, he was 1–3 with a 4.50 ERA. Although Nierko lost as many games as he won, his ERA was a tidy 2.82. In selecting him to pitch, Virdon was looking ahead to the end of the series in Los Angeles. He wanted both Ryan and Nierko available just in case he needed them to work with three days' rest.

Lasorda had already figured on Reuss to pitch the second game, regardless of whom Virdon decided on. The Dodger lefty wasn't at all popular with the Astro players. A week before, Reuss had thrown a fastball that hit Don Sutton in the knee. It shattered Sutton's kneecap and sidelined him for the rest of the playoffs. Sutton said he didn't think Reuss threw at him deliberately. Some of the Astros thought otherwise.

"We owe Reuss one because he hurt Sutton," said Scott. "No grudge or anything, but we have to get even. We don't need to throw at him or anything. The best way to get even is to beat him."

Howe, like Virdon, felt it was mandatory that the Astros win the second game so that they could go to Los Angeles with a big 2–0 advantage. He maintained that the team's playoff chances wouldn't be good unless they won the first two games. Garvey looked at it differently.

"If that's the way they're talking, it shows that they're worried," he reasoned. "It probably means they're in trouble."

Apparently Houston fans didn't feel the Astros were in danger. Fewer fans, 42,398, turned out for the second game. A couple of the more opportunistic ones unfurled a banner that read "Astros, watch your kneecaps."

Lopes watched Nierko's knuckleball flutter; he struck out to start the game. Baker fashioned a walk after Landreaux bounced out. Garvey made the third out by grounding out. Reuss didn't have any trouble with the Astros, setting them down in order.

The next time the Dodgers came up Scioscia singled, and Russell, who was dropped to eighth in the batting order, walked. However, Reuss, who was booed by the crowd, struck out to end the inning.

Again, Reuss retired the Astros in order. In the third, the Dodgers mounted an even more serious challenge. Lopes punched a single to right field and, after Landreaux popped out, Baker lined a single to center as Lopes held up at second. But they remained there as Garvey fouled out and Monday grounded out.

In the next two innings, all the Dodgers could produce was a single by Landreaux in the fifth. Meanwhile, Reuss was doing his job. He kept the Astros off the bases until the bottom of the fifth. After Cruz rolled to Lopes, Cedeno became Houston's first base runner by drawing a walk. Testing Scioscia's arm by stealing second, Cedeno was actually cut down by the rookie catcher's throw. Russell dropped the ball, however, and Cedeno was safe. Russell quickly made up for it. Dickie Thon, who had replaced Garcia at short, grounded a single into the hole between third and short. Russell dove for the ball and prevented it from going into the outfield. Cedeno, confident that he could score, ran past his third base coach's stop sign. Russell recovered and fired an accurate throw to Scioscia. The throw had the speedy outfielder beaten by ten feet. Cedeno slammed into Scioscia who held onto the tag for the third out.

Los Angeles generated another threat in the sixth. With one on, Monday and Guerrero put

Houston's Phil Garner joyfully scores second game's winning run in 11th inning.

Game 2	1	2	3	4	5	6	7	8	9	10	11	Total
Los Angeles	0	0	0	0	0	0	0	0	0	0	0	0
Houston	0	0	0	0	0	0	0	0	0	0	1	1

Mike Scioscia scrambles back safely into second base.

together back-to-back singles. After Scioscia flied out, Russell walked to load the bases. Then, on a full count pitch, Reuss struck out, killing the rally.

After Reuss surrendered the two-out single to Puhl before the Astros were shut down in the sixth, the Dodgers lost a golden opportunity in the seventh when Lopes doubled to start the inning. Playing for one run, Landreaux sacrificed Lopes to third. He died there, however, as Baker grounded to third and Garvey bounced to short.

After Reuss retired Scott to open the seventh, Cruz touched him for a single. In the process of fanning Cedeno, Cruz swiped second base. With first base open, Howe was given a free ticket. Lasorda preferred to take his chances with the light-hitting Thon. The strategy succeeded as Reuss got Thon on a

grounder to Garvey.

Reuss and Nierko had worked seven scoreless innings. It appeared that one run could provide the margin of victory. Nierko got the Dodgers out in orderly fashion but was lifted for a pinch-hitter in the Astros' turn at bat in the bottom of the eighth. Reuss again retired the side in order.

Dave Smith, who turned in a strong second half, took over for Nierko. He struck out two of the three Dodgers he faced in the ninth. Houston had an excellent chance to win the game then, as Garner opened with a single. After Scott popped to Garvey, Cruz hit safely to right as Garner stopped at second. But Reuss got Cedeno on a foul pop to Garvey, and Howe on a grounder. The tense contest would go into extra innings.

All the Dodgers could offer in the tenth inn-

98

ing was a two-out single by Garvey. Thomas, who had replaced Monday the inning before, struck out, and Howe came out of the Dodger bullpen to take over for Reuss. Thon greeted him with a single. He was bunted to second as the Astros positioned for a winning run. Still unwavering, Howe got rid of the final two batters.

Joe Sambito, another of Houston's fine relievers, came on to face the Dodgers in the 11th inning. He got Guerrero, but Yeager, pinch-hitting for Scioscia, drilled a double off the wall in left field. Russell negotiated a walk. The Dodgers needed a hit. Lasorda went to his bench. Smith batted for Howe and fanned. Mike Marshall hit for Lopes and also struck out as the Houston fans echoed their approval.

For the second straight day, Stewart came on in relief. He immediately got into trouble as Garner and Scott solved him for singles. That was enough for Lasorda. With runners on third and first, Terry Forster took over. The Dodgers had both their infield and outfield in, to cut off the winning run. Cruz hit a short pop to Baker and the runners couldn't move. Lasorda then called for rookie Tom Niedenfuer to replace Forster. Cedeno was walked intentionally to load the bases. The Dodgers were in a tight spot. Niedenfuer bore down and struck out Howe. It was a big out. He seemed to be out of danger as Denny Walling was sent up to hit for Thon. Walling looked over two pitches and then lined a single to right center, scoring Garner with the only run of the game.

Walling claimed that he noticed Niedenfuer playing shallow before he went up to bat.

"If teams keep playing us shallow, they're going to get burned," noted Walling. "We don't hit many homers, but we can hit line drives. When I saw it going over Thomas' head, it was absolute jubilation."

In a quiet Dodger dressing room Reuss explained why he left the scoreless game. He allowed only five hits and two walks in the nine innings he pitched.

"I went to Tommy, and I said, 'That's it,'" Reuss revealed. "I was beginning to get the ball up just a little bit. I'd thrown a lot of pitches. It was a tight ball game. In that situa-tion, you'd rather bring in someone fresh rather than have to work out of a jam. With all that was at stake in this game, you don't want to take the chance. You have to be honest with yourself. Part of me wanted to stay in there. I wanted to win this game as much as anybody."

Not more than Lasorda, who threw his shoe against the wall. . . .

GAME THREE

It didn't take a genius to see that the Dodgers were in deep trouble. In the two games—20 innings—they played with Houston, they had made just eleven hits and only scored one run. The team batting average was a lowly .157, which undermined two strong performances by Valenzuela and Reuss. Los Angeles was only one game away from being eliminated. It was a frightening thought.

Lasorda's original pitching plan was to use Bob Welch in the third game. That would have been fine if the Dodgers had managed to win one of the games in Houston. They hadn't. So, in a bold move, he switched to Burt Hooton as his starter and assigned Welch to shore up his fragile bullpen. Strategically, his thinking was sound. Welch, throwing hard in relief for two or three innings, would be balm for any ailment, nursing games along. Faced with extinction, Lasorda had to play it one game at a time now, using every arm available with the exception of the starting pitchers he was saving for games four and five.

"Tommy wanted an extra arm in the bullpen and Welch was the logical choice," explained Hooton. "We have to win. We can't hold anything back. We can't be thinking about [last] Saturday or Sunday. The Astros are a much better team than they were a year ago. Knepper and Sutton have strengthened their pitching, and Scott and Garner have helped them in the field. They have the defense to go with their pitching. The thing I feared most has happened: their pitching has stopped our hitting.

"There's no alternative but to go right after them. There's no way you can pitch conservatively. I'll go as hard as I can for as long as I can. The Astros can afford to be conservative.

Dusty Baker pulls up at second base with first inning double.

Game 3	1	2	3	4	5	6	7	8	9	Total
Houston	0	0	1	0	0	0	0	0	0	1
Los Angeles	3	0	0	0	0	0	0	3	x	6

We can't. That holds true for our offense and our defense. You ever see a dog that's backed into a corner? The only way out is to come right back at you."

Houston had to be thinking about their susceptibility in playing at Dodger Stadium. They had gone home empty handed after eleven of the twelve games they'd last played there. Just the year before, they had dropped all three games to the Dodgers, which brought about the memorable one-game playoff. Hooton, with his 11–6 record and a fine 2.28 ERA, had mastered the Astros over the year. He was 3–0 against them, and just two weeks before had spun a four-hit shutout in Houston. Knepper, who was originally scheduled to pitch the second game, was his opponent this time.

"I really and truly believe we're going to win three straight here again," said Lasorda.

After Hooton rejected the Astros in the first inning, the Dodgers struck quickly. Lopes opened with a walk. Landreaux bunted him to second, and Baker brought him home on a double. With first base open, Knepper pitched carefully to Garvey. He kept throwing breaking pitches. When he hung one high Garvey jumped on it, and lined a home run into the left field bleachers to give the Dodgers a 3–0 lead. The Dodger hitters had finally shaken their ennui.

Hooton didn't have any trouble in the second inning. However, Howe gave the Astros some life when he led off the third with a homer into the left field stands to cut the Dodgers' edge to 3–1. The Dodgers wasted a scoring opportunity when they came up as Monday bounced out with runners on third and first. In the fourth inning, they lost another as Landreaux fouled out to Cruz with teammates on second and first. It was the same pattern in the fifth. Again Dodger runners were on second and first, this time with just one out. But Monday fanned and Yeager bounced out.

All the while, Hooton was holding the Astros in check. He had a slight scare in the seventh when Cruz doubled with one out for Houston's third hit. Still, Hooton managed to get the side out without any damage. In the eighth, however, Hooton was through. After he issued a lead-off walk to Art Howe,

Lasorda brought Steve Howe into the game. Howe looked sharp as he struck out two of the three batters he faced.

The Dodgers were looking for some insurance runs off Sambito when they came up again. They hadn't made any offensive gains since the first inning. Guerrero opened up with a double. Thomas batted for Monday and was safe on a fielder's choice as Guerrero was thrown out at third. Yeager kept things going with a single. Then Russell came through with a single that scored Thomas for the Dodgers' fourth run. Meanwhile, Yeager advanced to third and Russell slipped into second on the throw to home.

Looking for a wedge to break the game wide open, Lasorda sent Reggie Smith up to bat for Howe. Smith flied deep to Puhl which allowed Yeager to tally the Dodgers' fifth run. After Lopes was walked intentionally, Landreaux cracked a single to score Russell. Baker ended the insurgence, but not before Los Angeles had ballooned its advantage to 6–1. Lasorda gave Welch a shot at wrapping up the victory. And Welch did it. The Dodgers were alive. They had it all today—pitching, hitting and defense. Later, in the Dodgers' clubhouse, Garvey was asked if he thought the Dodgers were now ahead psychologically though they were behind, 2–1, in games.

"That's a very good question," he answered. "Relative to last year, I think we're ahead now. All we have to win is three games in a row this year. Last year we had to win four."

Garvey's first inning homer had started them in that direction. It was his second of the series.

"Knepper had been throwing me breaking pitches," said Garvey, "and I wasn't really anticipating getting a good pitch to hit with first base open. He threw me a good curveball. It broke into me."

Despite limiting the Astros to just three hits, Hooton didn't feel he had done his best.

"Sometimes you feel like you have good stuff and you don't have to think about pitching," he said. "You can go after them with any pitch. My fastball, I don't want to say it was totally inconsistent, but it wasn't a fastball I felt I could challenge the hitters with. My curveball—the first two or three innings—I couldn't

Derrel Thomas slides safely into home in eighth inning.

get that over."

"I told them I believed more than anything in my life that we were going to win, and I wanted them to feel the same way," Lasorda said later of his pre-game speech to the players.

"Nothing we hadn't heard before," said Garvey. "And, believe, me, we've heard a lot before."

Nevertheless, nobody complained. . . .

GAME FOUR

Subliminal elements began to work on the Astros. They had to be thinking about a Dodger sweep. And why not? Los Angeles did it to them last year. Now they continued to dominate Houston in Dodger Stadium.

Maybe there *was* something to the superstition that the Astros were unflappable under the Dome, but unraveled at the smell of fresh air. Ashby, who had been the hero of the opening game victory, hinted at the factors that influence players' thinking.

"There are probably some jitters here," conceded Ashby. "Maybe there is a psychological factor. When the press keeps asking about it over and over, you have to think about it."

Sambito, one of Houston's better relievers, rationalized the psychology bit.

"There are other places where we don't play well," he pointed out. "We have problems in Philadelphia and in Pittsburgh. It's not just Dodger Stadium. They're a good team and they play well here. I think it's really as simple as that."

Baker congratulates Garvey on first inning homer.

"Maybe we are a little uptight here," said Cruz. "Maybe we try too hard. We have to relax."

The Astros couldn't afford to relax. They were going up against Valenzuela for the second time. This time they were facing Valenzuela without Ryan. Not wanting him to work with only three days' rest, Virdon elected to start Vern Ruhle instead. It was obvious that Virdon was looking ahead to the National League playoffs which began on Tuesday. Ryan didn't seem upset.

"With our staff, there's no reason to move me up," he said.

But Garvey felt the Astros were a bit uneasy.

"When they look at their record here, they have to be concerned," he said. "We play better in this park and they know it. Playing here has to put doubts in their minds, and that's to our benefit. They can afford to challenge you in the Dome. They have to be a little more cautious here. I'm sure if you ask them, they're concerned."

Valenzuela's appearance brought out the Latinos from East Los. A sold-out crowd of 55,983 turned out for the Saturday twilight game. The Dodger hitters were relieved that they didn't have to face Ryan's fastballs at that time of day, when it's hard to see them.

Valenzuela got the big crowd excited in the very first inning. He quickly disposed of the Astros in order, striking out the last two batters. He set them down again in the second, and in the third, and once again in the fourth. He had faced twelve batters and retired every one of them. Surprisingly, Ruhle did the exact same thing. Although he had a 4–6 record during the season, Ruhle was giving Valenzuela and the Dodgers all they could handle. Historians were now thumbing through the record books to learn the last time two pitchers were working on a no-hitter in the post season playoffs.

Cruz fouled out to Scioscia to begin the fifth inning. The troublesome Cedeno then got the game's first hit when he singled to left field. Valenzuela's bid for a no-hitter was gone. What was most important now was to keep bearing down in the scoreless game. Cedeno was threatening to steal when Valenzuela looked over at first and picked him off.

Cedeno broke for second but Garvey's throw to Russell beat him. Howe then bounced out to end the action.

Walling, who was the hero of the second playoff game, took over for Cedeno at first base when the Dodgers came up to bat. Ruhle got Garvey on a fly to left and struck out Monday. He had now retired all 14 Dodgers he faced. Dodger fans were getting edgy. Guerrero reassured them, bringing them to their feet cheering. He caught the pitch and sent it soaring into the left field stands to give the Dodgers a 1–0 lead.

It was up to Valenzuela now. He momentarily lost his control and walked Thon to start the sixth inning. The tying run was on first. Two outs later, Thon was on second on a sacrifice by Ruhle. Valenzuela left him there as he got Puhl on a harmless fly to Monday.

The Dodgers tried to extend their lead when Russell opened the sixth with a single. Valenzuela positioned him for a run by bunting him to second. When Lopes walked, the Dodgers had their biggest threat of the game going. However, Landreaux popped up and Baker forced Lopes, killing the rally.

Valenzuela sailed smoothly into the seventh. He retired the Astros in order. The way he was pitching, one run looked like it would be enough. But the Dodgers wanted to be certain. Garvey led off with a single, and was promptly sacrificed to second by Monday. The Dodgers were playing for an insurance run. Guerrero got a big ovation when he came up. This time he flied out. Virdon called time and went out to the mound to talk to Ruhle. They decided to walk Scioscia intentionally and take their chances with Russell. It backfired. Russell punched a single to right field that scored Garvey with the Dodgers' second run. Scioscia was cut down trying to reach third. It didn't matter because Valenzuela took a 2–0 lead into the eighth inning to the cheers of the crowd.

He got the first hitter, then Howe reached him for a single. Unruffled, Valenzuela retired the next two Astros to close the inning. It was of little consequence that Ruhle retired the Dodgers in order. Valenzuela was spinning a shutout and he had only one more inning to work.

Valenzuela carefully watches Scioscia make game-ending putout in Dodgers' 2–1 victory to even playoffs.

Game 4	1	2	3	4	5	6	7	8	9	Total
Houston	0	0	0	0	0	0	0	0	1	1
Los Angeles	0	0	0	0	1	0	1	0	x	2

He got Garcia, who pinch-hit for Ruhle, on an easy fly ball to Landreaux. However, Puhl lined a two-base hit up the alley in right center field. Valenzuela's shutout was in jeopardy. Garner, trying to go to right field, grounded to Lopes as Puhl ran to third. Valenzuela was one out away from a shutout. He didn't get it. Scott singled to left to score Puhl with Houston's first run. Lasorda yelled encouragement to Valenzuela as the dangerous Cruz came up. Calmly, deliberately, Valenzuela got Cruz to pop to Scioscia and walked off the mound with a 2–1, four hitter that evened the series at two games each.

Valenzuela's only anxious moment was in the ninth inning. Through all the excitement, Lasorda remained calm.

"There was no way I was going to take Valenzuela out of the game in the ninth inning," Lasorda declared. "It didn't even enter my mind. It didn't look as if he'd lost any of his stuff. He never ceases to amaze me. He was calm, cool and casual before the game while signing baseballs."

"Valenzuela appeared that way after the game, too.

"I think I have pitched better this year, but this was the team's most important game," he said. "I wasn't nervous. I prepared for the game like all the others. I don't know why I don't get nervous. It's probably just my natural way. I'll probably be more nervous tomorrow watching the game than I was pitching."

That's just the way Lasorda likes it. . . .

GAME FIVE

Neither Virdon nor Ryan thought about Tuesday. The playoff had been reduced to a one-game, winner-take-all affair. There wouldn't be a Tuesday if the Astros couldn't win the final game against the Dodgers. They were now looking over their shoulders at a team that had caught up with them after being one game away from elimination. Ryan had to face the fifth game knowing that he hadn't beaten the Dodgers in five tries in Dodger Stadium.

What buoyed Ryan's confidence this time was the fact that he had pitched a no-hitter and a two-hitter the last two times he had taken them on. That was enough for the smart money boys to make Houston the favorite to win the playoffs. The only trouble was that those two classic performances were spawned in the Astrodome. Now, on a sunny day in the Los Angeles air, it could be different. Ryan was their only salvation.

Ryan's mound opponent this time was to be Reuss. He had distinguished himself quite handsomely in the second game of the series by keeping his fastball low and never allowing a run in the nine innings he pitched, and it was a stylish match-up, even though Reuss didn't have Ryan's firepower. When Reuss has control of his pitches, he's as tough as anybody to beat. What it boiled down to was that Dodger hitters had to get to Ryan.

"Sometimes he throws it and you can't see it," said Lopes. "He just paralyzes you. He did it to Reggie Smith last year. He's throwing 95 MPH, you go to hit it and the ball pops up. You say adios, nice talking with you, that's one for you."

When Ryan began warming up in the bullpen before the game, the Dodgers were most interested. They knew he threw smoke. But to be completely effective, he has to have his curveball working. The fastball was there, all right, but Dodger instincts sensed he was having trouble throwing the curve where he wanted it.

There were 55,979 in the stands, wondering if the Dodgers would become the first team in playoff history to rebound from a 0–2 start and win the divisional championship.

Reuss opened smartly by setting down the Astros in the first inning. Ryan, too, began strongly by whiffing Lopes. After Landreaux flied out, Baker reached base safely on Garner's error. Ryan then got Garvey on a grounder to end the inning.

In the second inning Howe caused a scare with a deep fly to Monday. Cruz then dumped a single to left for the game's first hit. Reuss, keeping the ball low, got Walling to bounce to Lopes for what appeared to be a double play. However, Reuss dropped Lopes' throw and suddenly Houston had two runners on base. Reuss kept his pitches down and got Thon to hit to Guerrero. Trying for a double play, he

Garvey happily scores Dodgers' second run in sixth inning.

Game 5	1	2	3	4	5	6	7	8	9	Total
Houston	0	0	0	0	0	0	0	0	0	0
Los Angeles	0	0	0	0	0	3	1	0	x	4

Jose Cruz slides safely into second base in second inning.

threw to second to force Walling as Cruz moved over to third. Reuss eased the tension by getting Ashby on a grounder.

After Monday waved at a Ryan fastball, Guerrero walked. A moment later, he stole second. He made his way to third on Scioscia's grounder but died there as Russell flied out. Reuss walked Ryan, of all people, to start the third inning. Puhl forced him but later applied pressure by stealing second base. Two ground balls later the Astros still couldn't score.

The Dodgers muffed an excellent opportunity to score when they came up in the third. After Reuss struck out, Lopes smashed a hit off Garner's glove. Garner then picked up Landreaux's grounder and threw wildly, trying to nail Lopes at third. Running all the way, Landreaux reached second. The Dodgers had runners on third and second with only one out and their big hitters coming up. The fans cheered in anticipation of scoring at least a

run. That was the extent of it. Baker popped up and Garvey grounded out. The Dodgers came up empty.

The only action in the fourth inning was a two-out single by Walling. The Dodgers went out meekly. Both pitchers seemed in control. Ryan again held the Dodgers in check, fanning two more to bring his total strike-outs to six after five innings. He had retired the last eight Dodgers.

In the next inning Scott walked but then was caught stealing on a strong throw by Scioscia. It turned out to be a big play when Howe followed with a single. Cruz then worked Reuss for a walk before Reuss settled down and got the next two batters easily.

Ryan wasn't so fortunate. He made Landreaux his ninth straight out but walked Baker. Lasorda signaled for a hit and run with Garvey up. Three times Garvey fouled off pitches. Then, with the count 2–2, Garvey bounced a hit through short that enabled

Baker to slide safely into third. Confetti started to fall from the stands. The fans felt certain that the Dodgers would score. Ryan got ahead of Monday, 1–2. But then the veteran outfielder lashed a single to right field that brought Baker home with the first run of the game. Guerrero popped up to quiet things, then Scioscia created a racket with a single that scored Garvey. It wasn't over yet. When Walling dropped Howe's throw on Russell's grounder, Monday scored the third run. The Dodgers had pulled into a 3–0 lead.

Reuss could put it away now. He looked confident. Not even an error on Ashby, the lead-off batter in the seventh, could unnerve him. Ryan was through. When the Dodgers came to bat, Smith replaced him. Landreaux got a one-out double, and LaCorte took over. After Baker flied out, Garvey chased Landreaux home with a booming triple to left field. Reuss was sailing on a 4–0 lead.

Nothing could stop him now. He was touched for a harmless single in the eighth but struck out two of the three batters he retired. He kept pouring it on. He held the Astros in the ninth, dramatically striking out Roberts to end the game and send Los Angeles into the National League Championship playoffs. It was an extraordinary comeback. The Dodgers had won the distinction of being the first team to win a five-game playoff series after having lost the first two games. Lasorda almost flew to the mound, and fans poured onto the field.

Champagne corks popped all over the Dodger clubhouse. Howe doused Garvey's head with a can of beer, soaking the Brooklyn Dodger T-shirt Garvey was wearing. Reuss was speechless with joy.

"I really can't put into words how I feel," he said. "I guess it was like the no-hitter, but I couldn't put that into words, either. I don't think my stuff was too good out there. The ball was all over the place. The ball was jumping around. I might just have been too damn excited.

"Nolan pitched well. He wanted it just as much as I did. I knew it was going to be tough. But I knew if we got a few, that I could hold them. The three runs didn't hurt. When we got that field goal, I was happy as hell."

Scioscia had the best view of Reuss' pitches.

Pedro Guerrero hugs pitcher Jerry Reuss on his fifth game victory.

"The last couple of innings Jerry was in command," said the rookie catcher. "He'd gotten it all together by then. He was very strong, maybe too strong. He pitched his kind of game; he challenged the hitters."

Virdon, for one, had praise for the performances turned in by the Dodger pitchers.

"I attribute this series win to the Dodgers having outstanding pitching," said the Houston manager. "That's the reason we didn't hit. We're a better hitting club than we showed. I don't think you can go anywhere and see pitching back-to-back like you saw in this series."

"I believe in something called the last breath," said Baker. "You haven't beaten people until you've taken away their last breath. We were still breathing, even after we lost those first two games."

They had to save their breath for Montreal. . . .

MONTREAL PLAYOFFS

Dodger Stadium was tranquil the day after the Dodgers clinched the divisional playoffs. Just 24 hours earlier, the Dodgers had become the first team in the history of the sport to ricochet from a 2–0 deficit and win a playoff. So, if the players went almost casually through the motions of their afternoon workout, no one said anything.

The one serious moment for Lasorda came when he had to determine Ron Cey's ability to play in the upcoming games. For the past five days the pudgy Penguin, as Lasorda fondly refers to him, had been working out, testing his broken wrist, without really going all out. Originally the cast was to have remained on his left wrist for a period of five weeks. After just three weeks, however, Cey told his doctor that he felt good enough to play. X-rays revealed that the wrist was mending nicely and that even calcium was detected.

At first Cey experimented with two plastic casts. He used a large one on his forearm for batting, and a smaller one, over the point where the wrist was actually broken, when he played third base. Before his injury, Cey was enjoying one of the best seasons of his career. He had belted 13 home runs and knocked in 50 runs in just 85 games. His .288 batting average was the best he had ever compiled and he topped the club with nine game-winning hits. If the Dodgers wanted to play long ball, they needed Cey's bat in the lineup.

"I feel it's time to go," said Cey after a final workout. "I have done my work, and now I'm in a position to take advantage of it. I'm ready to dive for balls. I won't know 'til it happens, but I'm ready. I took a real crasher on my arm in practice the other day. It hurt, but nothing was broken. But I'm ready. There's still some pain, but it's subsiding. It will get better once I start playing again. I figure I'll be able to handle the physical end; and if I can't, I'll do it with positive thinking."

Actually, Cey had been working on the psychological part for the past several days. He had received special permission to dress and sit on the bench during the final three games against the Astros. Some observers may have thought he was sunning himself when they saw him sitting on the top step of the dugout. But Cey offers a disclaimer.

"I was concentrating on each pitch, trying to get ready."

Now he was ready. Lasorda was very thankful. He is fond of Cey and respects his ability as a player. With Cey's return Lasorda would be able to return Guerrero to the outfield.

"The Penguin can get hot; he gives us a little more defense at third base," said Lasorda.

Monday, who also was affected by Cey's return, felt the same way.

"The Penguin feels he's ready to hit," he said. "There's no question we're a better club when the Penguin is at third base, although Guerrero has done a good job too."

The Dodgers could definitely use more hitting. In the five game series with Houston, the team batting was a weak .198 (though it was still higher than Houston's figure of .179). Dodger pitching had made the difference. Reuss, Valenzuela and Hooton had held the Astros to an anemic six runs and 29 hits in the five game set. It wasn't lost on Virdon.

"If the Dodgers continue to get the kind of pitching they had against us, they'll beat Montreal and anyone else they have to play," said the Houston manager.

If Houston had been haunted by the thought of playing in Dodger Stadium, Montreal must have been near panic. In the 19 times they had played there, the Expos could only claim a single victory! To split just one of the two games against the Dodgers would have been a major triumph for Montreal.

The Expos hoped the achieve this with the return of two of their star players, Tim Raines and Rodney Scott. Both had been sidelined during September's closing race, when the Expos clinched first place in the second season. Neither had appeared in the five game series against Philadelphia. Their return provided Montreal with two sources of blazing speed.

Raines, a switch-hitting rookie outfielder, had an exceptional year. Not only did he hit .304, but he stole 71 bases in 82 tries before breaking a small bone in his right hand on September 13.

Despite a low batting average, Scott is a steady second baseman who also is a switch-hitter. In 1980 he stole 63 bases, and he had 30 in '81 before he injured his shoulder.

Raines and Scott are the first two batters in the order; they provide instant acceleration ahead of the club's long ball hitters, Andre Dawson, Gary Carter and Larry Parrish, which accounts for their importance to the team.

"Raines took batting practice on Sunday for the second straight day and will be ready for the Dodgers," reported Montreal manager Jim Fanning. "Scott took infield practice the same day and will also be ready to play."

The schedule formula for the National League Championship Series was reversed for the Dodgers. They were listed to play the first two games at home and then to play the final three games of the series in Montreal. Although the Expos didn't have the pitching quality of the Astros, they had more batting power. Dawson, who had hit .302 so far that season, led the team in homers with 24 and knocked in 64 runs. Carter had belted 16 homers and was the RBI leader with 68. Parrish was next with 44 runs batted in, and Warren Cromartie had hit .304, driving in 42 runs. Like the Dodgers, they worked with what was basically a three-man rotation led by Steve Rogers, their best pitcher, Scott Sanderson, Ray Burris and at times, Bob Gullickson.

"I don't think our guys will be thinking about what happened in the past here," said Fanning. "There were all kinds of things to think about in the final game against Philadelphia, Steve Carlton never having lost two games in a row and such."

GAME ONE

The 1981 championship was an historic event. Baseball's archives will record it as the first pennant that was decided on international soil. This was also the first time, in the 13 years of their existence, that the Expos had made it into the National League pennant playoffs. Furthermore, it was significant, at least to the citizens of Montreal, that the Expos accomplished the feat amidst a tumultuous upheaval within their ranks. As late as August, while the Expos were floundering with a 14–12 record, Dick Williams, the manager, was fired.

That was only half of it. Williams was replaced by the club's vice president of player development, Jim Fanning, a former catcher

Montreal outfielder Jerry White hangs on to fence and watches Scioscia's eighth inning home run go over the fence.

Game 1	1	2	3	4	5	6	7	8	9	Total
Montreal	0	0	0	0	0	0	0	0	1	1
Los Angeles	0	2	0	0	0	0	0	3	x	5

who hadn't managed anybody in 20 years. Even then Fanning had only been manager of a Class C minor league team in Eau Claire Wisconsin. Figure that one out. Even Fanning couldn't.

In his first three games as manager, Fanning lost every game. Somehow he turned it around after that. Montreal then won 16 of their last 24 games to win the second half of the Eastern Division standings with a 30–23 record, one game ahead of St. Louis.

Fanning decided to open against the Dodgers with righthander Bill Gullickson. Although the staff's ace, Steve Rogers, had pitched on Sunday, Fanning's selection of Gullickson was somewhat surprising. The 22-year-old was 7–9 for his season's work, which wouldn't strike fear in anyone. It was only his second year in the majors and what everyone remembered about him was that he had once struck out 18 Chicago batters in his rookie season. What influenced Fanning's thinking, however, was that Gullickson had

come around in the second half of the 1981 season and won six games. He had more confidence in Gullickson since Gullickson defeated Philadelphia in one of the playoff games. Still, the pitcher was years of experience away from Hooton, who looked strong after firing a three-hitter against Houston.

It didn't make any difference to the Dodgers who they faced. They had been veterans of post season play long before the Expos were involved. Experience breeds confidence, and the Dodgers weren't lacking in either area.

"Right now," said Monday, "you could bring in the 1927 Yankees and it wouldn't matter. We are sky-high."

"Montreal is tough," Baker added, "but we feel now that we can beat anybody. We lost the first two games last week and still came back and won three straight from a good Houston team."

Not that the Expos weren't exuding some confidence themselves. They had come back

Dusty Baker makes a diving catch in eighth inning.

114

against Philadelphia after winning the first two games and then being extended to a fifth.

As Parrish put it, "Down home in Florida I do some hog hunting, and we're like the hog. He'll run till you back him into a palmetto patch. Then he'll come out fighting."

After a scoreless first inning, Garvey led off the second inning with a single. The crowd of 51,273 gave Cey an ovation when he stepped in to hit for the first time since September 9. It didn't take long for him to show them how glad he was to be back. He sent a 3–2 fastball down the right field line that carried to the corner for a double and enabled Garvey to score all the way from first base. Gullickson got Guerrero on strikes, but Scioscia cracked a single that sent Cey to third. Dodger fans screamed for more runs and so did Lasorda. With Russell up, he ordered a suicide squeeze. Russell executed it perfectly, and Cey raced home with the Dodgers' second run.

Few suspected that the brief offensive outburst would be the extent of the excitement, but it was. Gullickson settled down and matched Hooton. Neither team seriously threatened the other over the next five innings. The only time the Expos got two men on base was in the sixth. Hooton turned back the challenge by getting Parrish on a pop to Scioscia.

Hooton did get a scare in the seventh inning. After Cromartie went out, Jerry White cracked a double to right. Chris Speier then hit a liner in the same direction, which first appeared to have "base hit" written all over it. However, Guerrero got a good jump on the ball and came in fast to make a waist-high grab. He lobbed the ball to Russell, to double White.

Hooton, the Dodger veteran, carried his 2–0 lead into the eighth, when he got rid of pinch-hitter Terry Francona, who batted for Gullickson. But a single by Raines brought Lasorda out to the mound. That was it for Hooton. Welch was brought in to check the Expos. He fanned Scott, the first batter he faced. However, Dawson got hold of one of his fastballs and sent it deep to left-center. Baker, running at top speed, dove for the ball and caught it just a few inches off the ground to save a sure double and a run.

Bill Russell avoids Montreal's Gary Carter.

Now it was Jeff Reardon's turn to control the Dodgers. He took care of the first two batters, Baker and Garvey, without difficulty. Then Cey ruffled his feathers with a single up the middle. The crowd applauded Cey as he left the field for Derrel Thomas, a pinch-runner. Thomas didn't have to run hard. Guerrero belted one into the left field bleachers to give the Dodgers a 4–0 lead. A moment later, it was 5–0 as Scioscia hit one over the right field fence.

Welch only needed three more outs. He didn't get them. Carter smacked a double to left center. When Parrish did the same thing, Lasorda motioned for Howe to take over for Welch. Howe was greeted with a single to center by Cromartie, but he stopped Parrish at third. Suddenly, the Expos had come alive, and Howe pounded his glove. He got White on a pop to Lopes, though, then closed the door by getting Speier to bounce into a game-ending double play.

Despite his strong performance, Hooton wasn't altogether happy with his pitching. Though he allowed only one run in 14⅓ innings of playoff pitching, Hooton is a perfectionist who always demands a great deal of himself.

"I didn't have any real good stuff," he admitted. "I made a lot of bad pitches, but not many of them hurt me. The guys behind me made sure of that. I was lucky."

"Usually in the warm-up pitches I can tell," added Scioscia. "I had an idea when he almost threw one over my head. He said he was throwing fastballs, and I thought they were changeups. That was when I had an idea. But I've seen him so many times without his overpowering stuff. The guy knows how to pitch. Anyone can go out with good stuff and win. A guy who wins with mediocre stuff, that's a good pitcher.

"Our pitching has been unbelievable. I knew we had a good starting staff, but I never imagined they'd turn in so many great, great games. The pitching was consistent all year but it's peaking now along with the rest of the team. We're not getting a lot of hits, but we're bunching them together. This is exactly what you look for. We're coming together at just the right time. Now we've just got to keep it rolling."

Cey had just begun.

"I knew I was going to be okay," he said. "With each pitch I was feeling my way back."

He was, indeed. . . .

GAME TWO

Montreal hoped it would have a good luck charm working for it in the second game of the series. Donald Sutherland, the Canadian-born movie actor, would be there rooting for them. Sutherland, a passionate Expo fan, had attended every game, at home or on-the-road, since September 12 (that was the day Montreal took off on the hot streak that brought them into the Eastern Division title).

"I'm afraid to change my clothes," said Sutherland, dryly.

Despite their opening loss, the Expos didn't feel pressure. They weren't yet faced with a must-win situation, and looked to pitcher Ray Burris, who was 9–7 over the year, to even the Series.

"You want to take each game as it comes," said Carter. "The Dodgers dropped the first two at Houston and won. We feel like we could do the same thing if we have to. The Dodgers have had some magic here in Dodger Stadium; they've played extremely well against us. I feel we have the same kind of magic at Olympic Stadium."

Cromartie looked at the situation in much the same way.

"I wouldn't say it's a must-win, but it would sure help," he said. "We've still got to go across the border. If we were in Montreal, I'd say it would be a must."

Even though they had taken the opener, most of the Dodger players felt their team was flat. Garvey, for one, felt that way, and Lopes came right out and said it.

"We were flat, no question. Luckily it didn't hurt us. It was a very emotional series with the Astros, and it's difficult to keep that prolonged; hard to keep up for a long period of time. The atmosphere was not as keyed as I've seen it before. Maybe today we'll regroup. Hopefully, we'll be a little higher.

"Did you see some of those empty seats yesterday? I guess the fans are letting us know that they're still revolting from the strike. But something's wrong. Hey, somewhere else, I could understand. But a playoff game in Los Angeles—not a full house?"

The house was full tonight. Valenzuela was the Mexican magnet again. There's no telling how many fans the Dodgers would have drawn if the regular season hadn't been interrupted by the players' strike. Valenzuela missed at least 15 starts, which would have made the turnstiles click just that much more.

Raines greeted Valenzuela and his fans with a sharp single to left to open the game. Feeling frisky, however, he took too big a lead off first base and was picked off by Garvey, throwing quickly to Russell, who slapped the tag on Raines. Valenzuela then took care of the rest of the Expos.

The Expos, in turn, struck swiftly in the second inning. Parrish singled after one out. White then followed with another hit. Cromartie put the Expos in front with a double to

Dusty Baker is out at second base in sixth inning.

Game 2										
	1	2	3	4	5	6	7	8	9	Total
Montreal	0	2	0	0	0	1	0	0	0	3
Los Angeles	0	0	0	0	0	0	0	0	0	0

right that sent White to third. Valenzuela walked Speier to load the bases. A frown formed on Lasorda's face, but he gave a sigh of relief when Valenzuela struck out Burris. Still, Valenzuela couldn't get past the pesky Raines. This time Raines singled to right. White scored the second run, but Cromartie was cut down on a strong throw from Guerrero to Scioscia.

While Burris kept the Dodger hitters off stride, Valenzuela found his groove. He retired nine Expos in succession, keeping the score at 2–0. In the sixth inning, however, Montreal struck again. Dawson began it with a one-out single. Carter followed with another. As Dawson sped to third base, Baker threw wildly in an attempt to get him. The speedy Dawson kept running and scored Montreal's third run. Valenzuela had given up more runs in six innings against Montreal than he had in 17 innings against Houston.

The Dodger hitters still couldn't do anything against Burris. Garvey hit into a double play with two runners on base to kill a rally in the sixth. They wasted a lead-off single by Russell in the seventh and actually had a chance to tie the game in the bottom of the ninth. But Burris tenaciously hung onto his 3–0 lead.

After Baker flied out, Garvey dumped a single to center. The Dodgers then got a break when Speier booted Cey's double play grounder. Suddenly the Dodgers had the tying run at the plate. Burris looked Guerrero over, fully aware that a mistake to the power-hitter would be costly. Guerrero swung and sent a torrid liner toward short. Speier gloved the ball with one hand and tossed it over to Scott for a game-ending double play. It was a tough way for the Dodgers to lose a game.

Burris couldn't restrain his happiness. He sounded almost arrogant.

"I'm sure everybody came out tonight to see Fernando Valenzuela, but maybe they saw a new star," he said. "To pitch a playoff game was very satisfying. And to pitch on national TV with my mom and dad watching, well, it gives me a chance to make a name for Ray Burris.

Mike Scioscia puts tag on Expos' Warren Cromartie.

Pedro Guerrero goes head first into second base.

119

"I used to throw the ball by everybody, but I changed when my sinker started hitting too many bats. We haven't played too well here; so this naturally gives us a lot of confidence heading into Montreal."

Burris, who had a lifetime record of 73–83, had kept the Dodger hitters anxious all night with his assortment of curves, sliders and changeups. They never really hit him hard. Garvey knew it.

"His game plan was to change speeds as often as possible," Garvey said. "We've handled him before, but he pitched a very good game. You have to give him credit."

That was more than Andre Dawson had to say for Valenzuela.

"He's nothing special. There's nothing particularly outstanding about him, except that he's a rookie and he gets all that publicity and everything."

Valenzuela knew he hadn't been as sharp as he'd been in the past. He looked at his defeat philosophically.

"I've said it before. You can't win every game. I was getting behind some hitters, but what happened in the second inning could happen in any game. I tried my hardest."

He'd get another chance to try harder. . . .

GAME THREE

The Dodgers' 720-B Fan Jet was carrying strange-looking cargo. Flying to Montreal in mid-October isn't exactly like jetting to Vero Beach. The usual swim trunks or shorts or polo shirts were replaced by mittens, wool jackets and fleece-lined parkas. Is this any way to approach a baseball game? The Dodgers weren't sure, but were prepared to play in whatever conditions the found north of the border. If the Dodgers were going to win their 17th National League pennant, they would have to be prepared—and there was no way the Montreal Chamber of Commerce could lull the Dodgers into believing that the weather in their fair city was only a few Fahrenheits colder than New York.

Ron Fairly, who had played for a decade with the Dodgers in Los Angeles before his five years in Montreal, qualifies as something of an expert on the Canadian weather.

"The best way for me to describe the weather in Montreal is to tell you how the weather report went," Fairly says. "It's like the old story, is the glass half empty or half full? We had such bad weather in one stretch, they said, 'We're going to have scattered daylight, with intermittent sunshine.'

"I played one game at 34 degrees, but with the wind-chill factor, it was about 15 degrees. One guy was treated for frostbite—a fan. You know those heaters that blow out almost like a flame? We had two of those in the dugout in Jarry Park. There were a few weeks when we ran into the sauna and turned it up to about 270 degrees. We went in there, uniform and all. I remember one day when it was windy and cold. The next day, I woke up and it was crystal clear. I thought, 'Oh my gosh, a heat wave.' I walked outside and it was ten degrees. We didn't play that day."

The weather appeared to be more of a topic than the game itself. When the Dodger players picked up the newspaper on Friday morning they were greeted by a catchy headline in the *Montreal Gazette:* "Montreal Isn't L.A. But It Isn't Siberia Either, Gentlemen." By game time, the air was clear and cool. The temperature read 46 degrees—excuse enough for brandy drinkers.

Reuss, who had been magnificent in the post-season playoffs, was the Dodgers' starter. He had pitched 18 innings against Houston without allowing a run, and yielding only 10 hits. He was facing Steve Rogers, Montreal's best. In 17 2/3 innings against Philadelphia, Rogers had surrendered just one run; and though he was combed for 16 hits, he had beaten Steve Carlton twice. While the teams were being introduced to the 54,372 bi-lingual fans, Lasorda employed some Pennsylvanian psychology. He sent his players onto the field without jackets.

"This is our weather," Lasorda told his players. "This is just how we like it."

Lopes showed how much by starting the game with a base hit and kept warm by stealing second base. Unfortunately, no one sent him home. It wasn't until the fourth inning that the Dodgers scored. With runners on third and first, Cey hit a slow grounder to Parrish allowing Baker to score the game's

Ron Cey slides hard into second base just missing Montreal's Rodney Scott.

Game 3	1	2	3	4	5	6	7	8	9	Total
Los Angeles	0	0	0	1	0	0	0	0	0	1
Montreal	0	0	0	0	0	4	0	0	x	4

Ron Cey hits single in fourth inning to score Steve Garvey.

first run. Unfortunately, Guerrero and Scioscia left Garvey on second.

Apparently Reuss liked the weather too. He wasn't having any trouble with the Expos. Through the first five innings, he had only permitted two hits. In the sixth, however, his shutout came to an end. There were two outs when Dawson got the third safety off Reuss—a broken bat single to center. Carter then worked Reuss for a walk. Parrish promptly tied the game with a grounder between short and third. The next hitter, right fielder Jerry White, didn't pose a threat: he had hit only .218 during the season with a total of three home runs. But anything can happen in the playoffs. Reuss quickly fell behind 2–0. Pitching coach Ron Perranoski went out to check with Reuss. Satisfied, he returned to the dugout. Reuss dealt a fastball. White swung

and deposited it over the left field fence for a three-run homer that sent Montreal into a 4–1 lead.

Buoyed by the unexpected blast, Rogers got tougher. He disposed of the Dodgers easily enough in the next two innings. In the ninth, however, he had a bit of a scare when Garvey and Cey hit back-to-back singles in an effort to start a rally. Fanning ran out to talk to Rogers. Guerrero swiftly killed it, though, grounding into a double play on a 3–1 pitch. When Rogers struck out Scioscia to end the game, the Expos had a 2–1 edge in the series.

It had never happened before. When White made his way into the clubhouse, a long row of white towels led to his locker. It was a tribute to a hero.

"This was my biggest hit," White said. "When Reuss is pitching me low, he's

Jerry White is mobbed following his game-winning three-run homer in sixth inning.

unhittable. I was just looking for something high. I knew the ball was over the fence just before I got to first base. I felt like jumping up and shouting."

Once White had put them ahead, Expo fans began to yell louder and louder.

"The fans had me so pumped up," said Rogers, "I thought I was Nolan Ryan, and I started throwing too hard. When Fanning came out to talk to me in the ninth, Carter told him, 'Don't you dare take him out.' "

Lasorda was annoyed. A bunch of exuberant Montreal fans made a point of dancing and yelling outside the Dodger clubhouse and he couldn't help but notice.

"I never heard of a team holding a damn celebration after winning two games in a row," he fumed. "They still have another game to win tomorrow, and they're not going to win. I've never felt so strongly in my life about winning."

GAME FOUR

Once more, the Dodgers found themselves with their backs to the wall, and a cold one at that. They were not accustomed to Canadian weather. They were not fond of losing either. They were in a strange city, cast as the underdogs. If there were Dodger fans in Montreal, none had appeared, and it was left to the Dodgers to psyche themselves up, on their own. They lacked the batting prowess needed to back-up their excellent pitching. In eight playoff games, they were hitting only .198 as a team. It was time to regroup.

Dusty Baker realized it. Before the start of Game Four he walked alone into Lasorda's office in the clubhouse and handed him a piece of paper. A short time later, Lasorda called his players together, and in the quiet of the clubhouse, read the message that was given to him. It was a scriptural quote, Romans, Chapter 5:

"Tribulations bring about perseverance; perseverance brings about proven character; proven character brings about hope and hope does not disappoint."

There were no amens. The players were taken aback. They remained quiet. Lasorda put the paper into his pocket and looked up.

He added a passage of his own. "That means that we all got to go out there and hope that we win."

It broke the tension. The players practically fell off their stools, laughing. They were loose, all right. Lasorda handed the ball to Hooton and told him to "Go get 'em."

Gullickson was Hooton's adversary once again. They had battled each other in the series' opener, when Gullickson turned in seven strong innings before departing. Hooton, like the other Dodger starters, was having an outstanding playoff. In the two games he won, he had pitched 14 innings, during which he had only allowed a single run. Hooton, a perfectionist, confided that he wasn't completely pleased with his work. No one considers him a daVinci but Hooton truly believes he should create a masterpiece every time he is called upon to pitch.

A crowd of 54,499 had turned out, convinced that before the sun set the Expos would hoist their first pennant above the city of Montreal. The day was sunny and the temperature, although not exactly comfortable, was 52 degrees. Since it was a day game, it would be somewhat warmer than the night before.

"It was really nice last night," Rogers smiled. "In April, when they had to thaw out the infield with blow torches and you had to run from the dugout to the infield on ice—that was cold. This hasn't been bad."

As he had the night before, Lopes opened the game with a single. The Expos had apparently forgotten that Lopes had stolen second the night before, because he did the same thing again, in broad daylight. Playing for a quick run, Russell bunted him to third. All to no avail. Baker's fly to center field was too shallow for Lopes to score, and Garvey fanned out for the third out.

The Dodgers missed a bigger opportunity to score in the second inning. Cey began it with a walk. Monday, making his first start in the series, singled to right as Cey stopped at second. Guerrero's drive to right enabled Cey to advance to third. Scioscia, however, smacked into a double play, to end the threat. Finally, with two out in the third, the Dodgers scored a run. It happened quickly. Russell was

Davey Lopes steals second in opening inning of fourth game.

Game 4	1	2	3	4	5	6	7	8	9	Total
Los Angeles	0	0	1	0	0	0	0	2	4	7
Montreal	0	0	0	1	0	0	0	0	0	1

safe on an error by Parrish who threw low to first. Baker then sent him home with a double.

Cey singled to open the fourth, but Guerrero grounded into a double play one out later. In the bottom of the inning, the Expos tied it. With one out, Cey booted Carter's grounder. Hooton got Parrish on a foul pop but then walked White. Cromartie then singled to deliver Carter with the tying run.

It didn't look as though the Dodgers would score again after forfeiting an almost certain chance to do so in the sixth. Baker had worked Gullickson for a walk when Garvey singled to center, enabling Baker to race to third. Cey then grounded to Parrish. Baker proceeded to break for home but was tagged out after colliding with Carter, who grimly held onto the ball. Given a reprieve, Gullickson struck out both Monday and Guerrero.

The score remained at 1–1 when Los Angeles came to bat in the eighth. After Russell fanned, Baker singled. Garvey, who thinks "long ball" in the late innings, homered over the left field fence to send the Dodgers into a 3–1 lead. Hooton finally had an advantage. Unfortunately, he weakened it a bit. When the Expos came up, Scott reached for a single. One out later, Carter did the same thing. At that point Lasorda removed Hooton and brought in Welch to quiet the Expos. Welch came through, striking out Parrish and getting White on a fly ball.

Dodger bats came alive again in the ninth inning. Yeager, hitting for Scioscia, opened with a hit. Derrel Thomas, who had entered the game as a defensive replacement the inning before, bunted safely. Lopes sacrificed both runners along. With first base open, Russell was given a walk. Baker then chased Yeager and Thomas home with a bouncer up the middle. Garvey flied out, but Cey kept the uprising going with a single that scored Russell. Lasorda then turned to Reggie Smith to pinch-hit for Welch. Smith came through with a hit that scored Baker and sent the Dodgers soaring into a 7–1 lead. They had produced their biggest inning of the playoffs, scoring four times. Howe came on in relief and made quick work of the Expos. The Dodgers had evened the series, 2–2.

Garvey had produced a home-run that broke the tight game open. He responds well to challenges.

"I was looking for something I could drive," he said. "Late in the game, that's what I try to do in the kind of situation we were in. I went up there looking for a slider. Gullickson had been starting me off with sliders and keeping them down. The pattern has been not to throw me a fastball with men on. So, I was looking for a slider. But he got this one up a little bit, and I was able to hit it out. A pitcher like Gullickson is a hard thrower, and he has a tendency to lose some speed as the game goes on. After the sixth inning against a pitcher like that, I look to drive the ball hard."

Hooton admitted that he'd been a little annoyed at his teammates' watered-down batting.

"I was a little perturbed at my own hitters for all the opportunities they were wasting," he said. "It was a little frustrating but maybe it kept me going. Maybe I relaxed a little after Steve hit that homer. I felt if I could get this win and get the team to Fernando, we'd be in pretty good shape."

GAME FIVE

The inevitable happened. The threat of bad weather, which had players and fans worried even before the first game was played in Montreal, became a reality. A cold and windy rain buffeted the city, causing the postponement of the fifth and deciding game for the National League pennant. Still, the league's officials were determined to hold the game. Telephone circuits were kept busy with frequent calls to the local meteorologist.

The weather served to emphasize what a hearty bunch of fans the Expos have. They sat in the half-filled stadium and sang, hoping for the game to begin. Actually, Montreal fans love to sing, and had done so in between innings in the first two games.

Finally, after waiting for close to three-and-a-half hours, league president Chub Feeney buttoned up his raincoat, turned up his collar and called the whole thing off.

Looking on the bright side of that gloomy day, a rescheduling to Monday meant that Valenzuela would get an extra day of rest. He

Ron Cey falls away from inside pitch.

had been pitching with three days of rest between starts, a schedule that would take its toll after a while. Of course, Burris would also benefit from the added day's respite. The only real drawback would be that the winning team would be denied a day off before the World Series, which was scheduled to start in New York on Tuesday.

The day-long rain ushered in cold weather. When action was scheduled to resume on Monday afternoon, the temperature was 41 degrees and the artificial turf was frosty. Monday was a work day, and only 36,491 fans felt the game was more important than a day at the office.

"I woke up this morning thinking I would be pitching the first game of the World Series," said Burris. "I'm not going to feel any pressure in this game. I'm going out there, trying to win. My last outing against this club speaks for itself. Someone will go on and someone else will go home. There will be no pressure on me. The only thing I'm putting on myself is my uniform."

Valenzuela wasn't feeling pressure either. He sat calmly on the Dodger bench after he finished his warm-up, chewing bubble gum and blowing bubbles. He just needed some hitting support—even half of what the Dodgers produced on Saturday.

As Baker put it, "Burris is a ground ball pitcher, and in this stadium it's either going to go in our favor tremendously or it's going to go against us. If the balls go through on the Astroturf, it'll be in our favor. Otherwise, the grounders will be right at them and you're going to see a lot of double plays."

Garvey liked the Dodgers' chances. He'd had a good playoff.

"The momentum has switched to us," he said. "We are a team that's been through adversity. We did it against Houston. We did it on Saturday against Montreal. And, with Fernando pitching, we are absolutely confident."

It looked like the Dodgers would score their very first time at bat. With one out, Russell went the opposite way on a Burris fastball and sent it down the right field line for a triple. The next two balls, however, never went more than 90 feet. Baker grounded to third and Garvey hit back to the box. The Dodgers couldn't bring Russell in.

Montreal didn't waste their chance when they came to bat. Raines clubbed a double into the gap in left center field. Positioning for a run, Scott bunted. Valenzuela tried to catch Raines at third, but the quick outfielder slid in safely. Dawson then hit into a double play as Raines came home. The Expos got on the scoreboard first.

Valenzuela then found his groove. He retired eleven batters in a row before Carter touched him for a two-out single in the fourth.

The Dodgers finally got a run in the fifth. Monday opened with a single and moved around to third on Guerrero's safety. Scioscia lined out to Scott. Then a wild pitch enabled Guerrero to reach second. And Valenzuela helped with a grounder to Scott that scored Monday with the tying run.

Valenzuela retired the Expos in order in the fifth and sixth innings, and he got the first two in the seventh. Of the last 20 batters he'd faced, he had retired 19 of them. Parrish then upset his momentum with a double. Lasorda ordered White walked intentionally. Valenzuela then got Cromartie on a pop for the third out, and in the eighth he picked them off in order.

When the Dodgers came up in the ninth, Rogers was waiting for them. Fanning brought in his ace pitcher after Rogers pinch-hit for Burris the inning before. It was his first relief appearance in three years. He got Garvey on a pop. Cey hit deep to left but not far enough, for the second out. Monday was up next. He fell behind, 3–1. Figuring that Monday was taking, Rogers grooved the next pitch. It was too good to pass up. Monday swung and sent the ball just to the right of the center field fence. Dawson and White ran back, then stopped and watched helplessly as the ball went over for a home run. There was no singing in the stands now. The Dodgers were on top, 2–1.

Valenzuela got the first two Expos in the bottom of the ninth. Then he walked Carter. Lasorda called time and went out to check with Valenzuela, who again tried for the third out. He failed, issuing a second consecutive walk, this time to Parrish. That was it for the

Fernando Valenzuela watches as a wild pitch gets away from Gary Carter.

Game 5	1	2	3	4	5	6	7	8	9	Total
Los Angeles	0	0	0	0	1	0	0	0	1	2
Montreal	1	0	0	0	0	0	0	0	0	1

Rick Monday hammers game-winning ninth-inning homer.

sensational Mexican rookie. Lasorda brought in Welch to get the final out. White, up next, was all that stood in the way of a Dodger pennant; and Welch got him on a grounder to Lopes.

Champagne flowed freely in the Dodger dressing room. Monday, drenched, took a long swallow, then came up for air.

"I was surprised he gave me a good pitch—a waist-high fastball over the middle of the plate," he said. "After I hit it, I didn't know where it went. I saw the outfielders going for it. I finally caught sight of it just before it sailed over the fence. I almost fell down between second and third. I should have done better with the first pitch he threw me. I

fouled it off and thought, 'I'll never see one that good again.' The way Burris had pitched and with the success that Rogers has had, I wouldn't have expected to see one again."

Valenzuela had earned his share of champagne, too. He had been in total control after the first inning until two-out in the ninth. He'd tried too hard to finish.

"I wasn't really tired in the ninth," he explained through an interpreter. "I was just putting a little extra on my pitches and that got me in trouble. I feel glad to have reached the major leagues and helped the Dodgers reach a World Series."

Lopes said it for all the Dodgers. "Now we have a score to settle with the Yankees."

Valenzuela shows his championship form.

THE DODGER-YANKEE RIVALRY

There was no time for merriment. Happy, but weary, the Dodgers couldn't fully savor their dramatic National League pennant victory over the Montreal Expos. Normally, they would have enjoyed an extra day to spend toasting Rick Monday on his ninth inning home run before beginning World Series play. However, a snowy Sunday's postponement of the fifth and deciding game against the Expos to Monday had eliminated that luxury. Instead, the entire Dodger entourage had to rush for a plane Monday evening and fly to New York for the opener on Tuesday. The 1981 World Series' blueprint listed the first two games in New York, the next three games in Los Angeles and the final two back in the Big Apple.

The Dodgers and Yankees were no strangers to each other in the World Series. In fact, the ghosts of games past linger on to haunt the Dodgers. Now they were facing the Yankees for a record-setting eleventh time with the sour emptiness a person feels the morning after an all-night binge. In ten previous encounters, the Dodgers had only won twice. Diehard Yankee fans gloated loudly over this fact.

Despite the Yankee's domination, the au-tumnal play between the two adversaries has produced more than its share of World Series thrills. Crusty Brooklyn Dodger fans, still loyal to the memories of Ebbets Field and the spirits of their beloved Bums, as they were affectionately known, can recall with bittersweet accuracy the excitement generated in earlier years by a contest between these ball clubs. Veteran fans of the earliest campaigns go back to 1941, when the Dodger-Yankee rivalry surfaced for the first time. Back then, when it was safe to stand on street corners at night, arguments would last for hours over who was better; Pete Reiser or Joe DiMaggio; Billy Herman or Joe Gordon; Joe Medwick or Charlie Keller; Dixie Walker or Tommy Henrich; Pee Wee Reese or Phil Rizzuto; Mickey Owen or Bill Dickey; Cookie Lavagetto or Red Rolfe; Whit Wyatt or Red Ruffing; Hugh Casey or Johnny Murphy.

Remembering back 20 years, the Dodgers first appeared in the post season classic and the start of the 'Subway Series,' when for a nickel one could travel from the Bronx to Brooklyn. That Series is best distinguished by a ninth inning strikeout in the fourth game that started a game-winning rally by the Yankees. After the teams had split identical

3–2 games in Yankee Stadium, the Yanks took the opening game at Ebbets Field, 2–1, in a closely played series in which all three games were decided by one run. The Dodgers appeared to be headed for a 4–3 victory when lightning struck after two outs in the final inning. On a 3–2 pitch to Henrich, the Yankee rightfielder was fooled by a curve ball. He swung and missed. It first appeared to be a game-ending strikeout by the Dodgers' ace reliever Hugh Casey. However, the ball got past Owen, and Henrich reached first base safely.

The break was all the Yankees needed. DiMaggio followed with a single to left and scored a moment later when Keller doubled high off the rightfield screen to give the Yanks a 5–4 lead. After Dickey walked, Gordon belted a two-run double that gave the Yankees a 7–4 win. The following day, it was all over as the Yanks swept all three games in Brooklyn, leaving Owen and Dodger fans with a lifelong nightmare.

"I was in the dugout holding a lot of the fellas' gloves—DiMag, Henrich, Keller, my own," recalled Rizzuto. "We didn't want to lose any of them when the game was over. When Henrich swung and missed, we all got up and started toward the runway that led out of the dugout. Some of us were already onto it. I know I was. Then we heard all that yelling, and we jumped back. There was Tommy running down to first base. Owen was chasing the ball over near his dugout. By the time he got it, Tommy was on first and there was no play."

It was the one play that Owen will be remembered for all his life. Yet, he had played in 128 games with the Dodgers that season after having been with the St. Louis Cardinals the year before. In all those games, he committed only three errors and had been charged with just two passed balls. The one he'll never forget probably cost the Dodgers the Series, and he never once offered an excuse for his misplay.

"It was all my fault," Owen admitted. "It was a great-breaking curve, and I should have had it. It got away from me; and by the time I got hold of it near the corner of the dugout, I couldn't have thrown anyone out at first. It was like a punch on the chin. You're stunned.

Yanks' Joe DiMaggio slides home safely in ninth inning of fourth game of 1941 Series.

Jackie Robinson is caught in a rundown in 1947 Series.

You don't react. I should have gone out to the mound and stalled around a little."

In 1947, when the World Series was televised for the first time, the Yankees and Dodgers heightened the drama. Jackie Robinson became the first black player to participate in the World Series after becoming the first black ever to play in the majors the same year. Although he led the Dodgers with seven hits, he couldn't prevent the Yanks from winning a second time, four games to three. Still, it was a Series that provided other breath-taking moments.

One was the first pinch-hit home run in Series play, executed by rookie Yankee catcher Yogi Berra in the third game that was won by the Dodgers, 9–8. But it was in the fourth game, when the Dodgers were trying to even the Series, that excitement rocked Ebbets Field to its foundation. Yankee righthander

Bill Bevens, who was only 7–13 during the regular season, was pitching a no-hitter in a bid to become the first to do so in World Series history. Although wild, Bevens and the Yankees were leading, 2–1, when the Dodgers came up for the last time. Bruce Edwards flied deep to left, and Carl Furillo walked, the ninth batter to do so. When Spider Jorgensen fouled out for the second out, it appeared as if Bevens would be writing his name into the record books. Dodger Manager Burt Shotton then turned to his bench. He named Pete Reiser, who was hobbling with a leg injury, to bat for Casey and instructed reserve outfielder Al Gionfriddo to run for Furillo.

Berra was having a good Series defensively. Shotton's strategy was obvious; he would order Gionfriddo to steal. On a 2–1 pitch to Reiser, which was called ball three, Gionfriddo easily stole second base. Yankee Manager

Gil Hodges (14) leads Dodgers off field after 4–2 victory in opening game of 1952 World Series.

Duke Snider at bat in 1952 classic.

Joe Black pitched opening game win.

Billy Martin saved Yanks with dramatic seventh inning catch of bases-loaded pop by Jackie Robinson in seventh game of 1952 Series.

Bucky Harris then told Bevens to intentionally walk Reiser. As soon as Reiser hobbled to first base, he was replaced as a runner by reserve infielder Eddie Miksis. Leadoff hitter Ed Stanky was due up next, and Dodger fans anticipated another walk.

However, Shotton called Stanky back. Instead, he sent up substitute infielder Cookie Lavagetto to face Bevens. After taking a pitch, Lavagetto brought the crowd to its feet. He smacked a high, outside fast ball hard against the wall in right field. The carom zipped past Henrich while Gionfriddo and Miksis scored to give the Dodgers a 3–2 victory to even the Series at 2–2.

In the sixth game, with the Dodgers trailing in the Series, 3–2, the diminutive Gionfriddo preserved his team's 8–6 win with perhaps the most dramatic catch in Series history. Leading 8–5, Shotton sent in Gionfriddo as a defensive replacement in leftfield when the Yanks came up to bat in the bottom of the sixth inning. There were two out and two runners on base when DiMaggio came up to bat. He didn't wait long to bring the crowd of 74,065 to its feet. He swung at lefthander Joe Hatten's first pitch and sent it soaring toward the Yankee bullpen, some 415 feet from home plate. Gionfriddo took off and raced toward the belt-high railing that separated the grandstand from the bleachers. At the last split second, he leaped and gloved the ball just as it went over the fence. The large crowd gave Gionfriddo a thunderous ovation for a spectacular catch. However, the Yankees came back the next day to beat the Dodgers, 5–2, in the seventh and deciding game.

Two years later, the 'Subway Series' resumed and the Dodgers again came up empty-handed. They had two outstanding players from the Negro leagues; catcher Roy Campanella who hit .287 and belted 22 home runs during the regular season and pitcher Don Newcombe, who led the Dodger hurlers with 17 victories that included five shutouts. It was also the first year colorful Casey Stengel was manager of the Yankees.

The opening game was a classic pitchers' duel between the rookie Newcombe and the veteran Allie Reynolds. Although he had pitched only four complete games all season,

Reynolds appeared strong, striking out six straight Dodgers in the eighth and ninth innings of a scoreless game. Newcombe was equally overpowering. He had fanned 11 batters as he faced Henrich in the bottom of the ninth. Working carefully to the dangerous pull-hitter, Newcombe missed with his first two pitches. Henrich was waiting for another fast ball and got it. He promptly lined the ball into the lower rightfield stands for an exciting 1–0 Yankee triumph in what many consider one of the finest pitching battles in Series' history.

Dodger hopes were buoyed the very next day when Preacher Roe hurled a masterful 1–0 shutout. Brooklyn evened the Series and was now going home for the next three games. Dodgers hopes were short-lived. To their astonishment, the Yankees swept all three games at Ebbets Field to win for the third straight time over the Dodgers, 4–1.

In 1952, the Yanks and Dodgers were back at it again. Gone was DiMaggio, replaced by Mickey Mantle, an exciting switch-hitter who had shown great promise as a rookie the year before. Despite the fact that Snider whacked four homers and drove in eight runs during the Series, the Dodgers lost for the fourth consecutive time, 4–3.

Brooklyn Manager Charlie Dressen stunned the Yankees by starting his relief ace, Joe Black, in the opening game. Black, who was 15–2 during the regular season with a 2.15 ERA, went nine innings to beat Reynolds in the opener at Ebbets Field, 4–2. He was pitted against Reynolds in the fourth game and went seven innings, yielding only a run in a 2–0 loss. The drama was set in the seventh game with Black facing the Yankees for the third time. Black lasted 5⅓ innings and was touched for three runs in the Yankees' clinching 4–2 triumph. Mantle, who, like Snider, had ten hits in the Series, clubbed a game-winning homer off Black in the sixth inning to break a 2–2 tie, and delivered a run-scoring single for the Yanks' fourth run in the following inning.

Yet, it was Billy Martin who saved the game and the Series for the Yankees. In the bottom of the seventh inning, the Dodgers had a rally going. Raschi had replaced Reynolds and walked Furillo to start the inning. After Rocky

Carl Erskine is mobbed by teammates following his 14-strikeout victory over Yanks in 1953.

141

Johnny Podres celebrated his 23rd birthday with an 8–3 victory over Yankees in third game of 1955 World Series.

Nelson popped up, the Dodgers came alive. Billy Cox got a hit and Reese worked Raschi for a walk to load the bases and bring up the dangerous Snider. Stengal lifted Raschi and brought in lefthander Bob Kuzava to face Snider.

Dodger fans moaned when Snider hit a weak pop for a second out. They cheered for Robinson, the next batter, to get a game-tying hit. Robinson ran the count to 3–2 and then swung at a curve ball. He, too, popped up between first base and the pitcher's mound. First baseman Joe Collins seemed confused. Kuzava looked around and nobody in the Yankee infield seemed to take charge. Finally, with a burst of speed, Martin dashed in from the edge of the outfield grass and made a startling catch around his knees as two Dodger runners were about to score.

It was the same script the following year, only this time the Yankees did it in six games.

In so doing, they won the title for an unprecedented fifth consecutive time, which made the puckish Stengel a managerial genius. The Dodgers had achieved their third pennant in five years with a potent lineup that included five .300 hitters. Yet, it was a light-hitting Martin who was the hero of the Series. He hit an amazing .500 with a record 12 hits in six games, leading both teams with eight runs batted in.

After the Yankees won their first two games in Yankee Stadium, pitcher Carl Erskine temporarily stopped them with a record-setting performance before the Flatbush faithful. He struck out 14 batters to beat the Yanks, 3–2, in a tight pitchers' duel against Vic Raschi. It wasn't until the eighth inning that the Dodgers scored the winning run. Although the Dodgers won again the next day, the Yankees came back to take the next two games and the Series. Martin completed his heroics with a

Yanks' Don Larson pitched the first perfect game in World Series history in 1956.

Sandy Koufax baffled Yanks in 1963 Series.

game-winning single in the bottom of the ninth inning that gave the Yankees a 4–3 victory.

Finally, in 1955, it happened for the first time, and there was joy in Flatbush. After losing in all seven World Series in which they appeared, the final five going to the Yankees, the Dodgers, at last, succeeded in raising the World Championship flag over Ebbets Field. It took them seven games to accomplish it. They also became the first team in World Series to win the crown after losing the first two games. It was an unusual Series. Newcombe, who had a 20–5 record, still couldn't beat the Yankees. He lasted only 5⅔ innings in the one game he started. The Yankees won the opening two games in Yankee Stadium, lost the next three at Ebbets Field, finally won the sixth game only to fall prey to young Johnny Podres, 2–0, in the seventh and final game.

It was in the seventh game when that Series' most memorable play occurred. The Yankees were trying to overcome a 2–0 deficit in the bottom of the sixth inning. Martin opened the inning by drawing a walk and Gil McDougald reached base safely on a well-executed bunt. Next up was Berra, who was then the hottest Yankee hitter, collecting ten hits to lead both teams.

At the time, it didn't appear that the defensive moves that Manager Walter Alston had made before the Yankee half of the inning began would have any significance. In the Dodgers' turn at bat, Alston removed second baseman Don Zimmer for a pinch-hitter. In so doing, he was forced to bring in leftfielder Jim Gilliam to play second base and put Sandy Amoros in left. Berra was a notorious pull-hitter at the time. Although he was squatty, he also had power to right. Realizing it, Amoros played him more toward left center, leaving the leftfield foul line wide open.

Berra hit Podres' first pitch and sent the ball toward the leftfield line. It looked like a certain double that would tie the game. But the fleet-footed Amoros never gave up on the slic-

Yankees' Reggie Jackson hit three homers in one game against Dodgers in 1977 match-up.

ing liner. He caught up with the ball, stuck out his right hand and insured Podres' shutout and the Dodgers' first World Series conquest in eight attempts. The joyous Dodgers carried Podres off the field on their shoulders.

Brooklyn celebrated for three days.

But the following year, the Yanks and Dodgers were back at it. It was a significant Series in more ways than one. As it turned out, 1956 was to be the last time the Dodgers would play in Brooklyn, ending one of the most colorful and zaniest eras in baseball's history. The Series was also the last for Robinson. But

it will be remembered most for Yankee pitcher Don Larsen's flawless game, the first perfect World Series game.

The Dodgers tried hard to make their last Series appearance in Brooklyn successful. They won the first two games at home before moving over to Yankee Stadium for the next three. With the Series deadlocked at 2–2, Larsen made his second start in Game 5. In the second game, he had been clubbed for four runs in less than two innings before he was removed. But now, Larsen threw only 97 pitches in spinning his masterpiece and struck

out seven with his no-windup delivery. Three exquisite fielding gems saved Larsen's no-hitter. The first came in the second inning when Robinson lined a bullet off third baseman Andy Carey's glove. The ball bounced to shortstop Gil McDougald, who picked it up and quickly fired it to first base to nip the ond game, he had been clubbed for four runs in less than two innings before he was removed. But now, Larsen threw only 97 pitches in spinning his masterpiece and struck out seven with his no-windup delivery. Three exquisite fielding gems saved Larsen's no-hitter. The first came in the second inning when Robinson lined a bullet off third baseman Andy Carey's glove. The ball bounced to shortstop Gil McDougald, who picked it up and quickly fired it to first base to nip the speedy Robinson by half a step. Gil Hodges almost spoiled Larsen's bid twice. In the fifth inning, he drove a ball to deep left center where the fleet Mickey Mantle ran it down with a stabbing backhanded catch. Then in the eight inning, Hodges lined a shot that Carey speared with one hand.

Newcombe, who turned in an outstanding 27–7 record during the season, failed in his two attempts to beat the Yanks. In Game 2, he was raked for six runs in 2⅔ innings. And in the seventh game, with a chance to give the Dodgers their second straight championship, Newcombe was touched for five runs in the three innings he worked as the Yankees won easily, 9–0.

The Dodgers' second pennant in Los Angeles also resulted in their second World Series Championship there in 1963. The superior pitching that the Dodgers displayed all season long was never more apparent than in the Series. Led by lefthander Sandy Koufax, who had a remarkable league-leading 306 strikeouts and 25 victories, Dodgers pitchers simply overpowered the Yanks, allowing them only four runs and just 22 hits in the four-game sweep. Koufax won two of the games while Johnny Podres and Don Drysdale won the others.

Koufax's opening game triumph was a masterpiece. He set a new World Series strike-out record by fanning 15 before 69,000 fans in Yankee Stadium, breaking former Dodger Carl Erskine's mark of 14 set ten years before. Koufax set the mark dramatically. Leading 5–2 when the Yanks came up for the last time, Koufax had 13 strikeouts. He fanned pinch-hitter Phil Linz to open the inning and wrote his name in the record books by striking out Harry Bright to end the game.

"I knew I had tied the record when I saw the number fourteen flashed on the scoreboard," Koufax said. "And I debated with myself whether I should really go for fifteen. I'm such an admirer of Carl that I almost hated to take the record away from him."

After 1963, the Yankee Dodger rivalry faded for 14 years. It started again in 1977, and was continued the following year. In both years, the Dodgers were victimized chiefly by the slugging of Reggie Jackson, who, because of his hitting, earned the title, 'Mr. October.' Both Series went six games. In 1977, Jackson set a record with his prodigious home run production. In the sixth game at Yankee Stadium, one that will long be remembered, he belted three homers, all of them coming on the first pitch thrown to him by Dodger pitchers. Since he had hit another, his last time at bat in Game 5, Jackson actually hit four homers in four official times at bat. He set a record by hitting five home runs in a six game Series.

In 1978, it seemed as if the Dodgers just might sweep the Yankees. Davey Lopes borrowed a chapter from Jackson's home run book and smacked two of them in the Dodgers 11–5 opening game triumph. The next night, Bob Welch, in relief, fired a third strike past Jackson in the ninth inning to preserve a 4–3 win that left the Yankees in a hole.

However, returning to Yankee Stadium, the Yanks rebounded. They swept all three games, then went back to Dodger Stadium for a 7–2 clincher. Jackson continued his slugging, belting two home runs in the Series and batting in eight runs for the second straight year. The Yankees had won eight of the ten World Series meetings against the Dodgers, a mastery that left the Los Angeles team shaking their heads in disbelief. Lasorda and a number of his players wanted yet another crack at the Yankees.

They finally got it . . .

Davey Lopes hit two homers in one game in 1978 World Series.

WORLD SERIES

"I'd say it's going to be tough for the Dodgers in the World Series," remarked catcher Gary Carter of Montreal, whom many felt would face the Yankees. "It's going to be uphill."

The position was nothing new for Los Angeles. In the opening round, they quickly fell behind, dropping their first two games to the Houston Astros. With their backs up against Chavez Ravine, they rallied to sweep the next three games and advance into the championship playoffs. Although they beat Montreal in the opener, they dropped the next two contests and were only one game away from elimination. Once more they rallied and took the next two games, winning the pennant on Monday's dramatic home run on a cold day in Montreal.

The Yankees had been waiting for the World Series to begin ever since Saturday. They had disposed of the Oakland Athletics in three games in the American League championship playoffs and were loose and rested. Still, the Yankees weren't without off-field theatrics that owner George Steinbrenner somehow manages to orchestrate. Then, too, at Friday night's victory celebration in Oakland, Jackson and third baseman Graig Nettles

had a difference of opinion that ended up with 'Mr. October' on the floor. The incident was sure to spark the Yankee fans, who were boisterous enough the last time the Dodgers heard them during the 1978 Series. Some of the Dodgers remembered it all too well and were not exactly looking forward to appearing in Yankee Stadium.

"It was a pleasure to come into a city that presents and reacts to a series as Montreal did," said Monday. "We hope that's the case in New York, but we don't totally expect it. I don't like the park and I don't like the town. I don't understand their way of life here."

He had a sympathizer in Bill Russell. The Dodger shortstop didn't hide any feelings after the 1978 experience. This time, at least, the Dodger players knew what to expect.

"With 56,000 screaming people out there, it's hard to concentrate," said Russell back then. "The fans were unnerving. It's tough to play here. The people are obnoxious. They have no courtesy at all. They never let up on you. So many things are going on here it makes it tough to concentrate on the ballgame. But, of course, you expect it in New York. The writers are the worst; the fans are the worst and the city is the worst.

Yanks' third baseman Graig Nettles.

"We were a cocky young bunch of players back in 1977 and 1978," continued Russell. "They called us the Hollywood Stars. We thought of ourselves as intimidators. This year, we are all a few years older. We knew we really couldn't intimidate anyone anymore. To compensate for that, we had to prove to others that we, ourselves, simply couldn't be intimidated by anyone. Or by any situation."

It was obvious this Series meant more than any of the others. The Dodger veterans—there were about ten of them on the squad who had swallowed the bitter pill of defeat the last two times—wanted to taste the nectar of the gods. There would be no next time for them and they knew it. One of them, Davey Lopes, put it in perspective.

"We had the ability to blow people away in those days," Lopes said. "This year, we had to rely more on the unexpected for success . . . the stolen base, the extra base on a single, the hit and run, and so forth. But our desire to win is greater in 1981. This team has more character.

"A lot of people are saying that this is the last year our infield will be together. We got to the World Series twice before with this unit, but we never won with it. This year is a kind of last hurrah for us. I've said it before and I'll say it again: If we can win the Series, they can do anything they want with us next season. A lot of people have given up on us all year, from top to bottom, inside and outside. But here we are. We're in the World Series. After we win it all, I don't care what they do."

It was almost as if Lopes was issuing a challenge to the Dodger hierarchy. He had heard the rumors. He would be 36 before the 1982 season was a month old. Ron Cey would be 35 and Garvey and Russell would both be 34. It was hardly the youthful infield you build a future on. That's why this Series meant so much. There were no tomorrows.

Despite their previous success against the Dodgers, the Yankees didn't take them lightly. Reggie Jackson, who is so much a part of the Yankee-Dodger legend, knew it. Because of a strained calf muscle, the dangerous slugger was listed as questionable for the Series opener. In fact, it wouldn't be known until game time if Jackson could play. Since there was no designated hitter this time around, Jackson would have to play the outfield as well as swing a bat. After the Yanks' final workout the day before the opener, Jackson talked seriously about the Dodgers.

"We've got to know that this is going to be a tough Series," Jackson said. "I'm just leery because we've beaten the Dodgers twice, but it's tough to beat a good team three times. It's going seven games. At least six. They are good. They're just like us. They do everything well, and they've got good starters. And they'll be more prepared for the task. Mentally, they will be more prepared."

What the Dodgers were prepared to do was rely on the left-handed pitching of Valenzuela and Jerry Reuss. It didn't escape Lasorda and the Dodger braintrust that the Yankees were only 25–25 against lefty starters over the season. In Valenzuela and Reuss, Los Angeles possessed two of the top lefthanders in the National League. Since Valenzuela pitched the last game in Montreal, the earliest he could pitch again would be in Game 3 on Friday when the Dodgers would return home for the three games slated for Los Angeles.

Lasorda's choice to open the Series was elementary. He picked Reuss who was 10–4 for the season with a fine 2.29 ERA. Yankee manager Bob Lemon had any number of choices from a well-rested pitching staff. He named Ron Guidry, a lefthander who was 11–5 with a 2.76 ERA, saving Tommy John to face Burt Hooton the next night. Late Monday night the oddsmakers established the Yankees as 8–5 favorites to beat the Dodgers. By game time on Tuesday night, the odds had risen to 9–5. The nation's bookmakers were getting a lot of play on the Yankees.

Danny Sheridan, a leading national football and baseball analyst in Mobile, Alabama, didn't agree. When contacted by sports announcer Bud Furillo of radio station KABC in Los Angeles, Sheridan made his sentiments known.

"Who do you like?" asked Furillo.

"The Dodgers," answered Sheridan.

"You really mean it?" shot back Furillo.

"Most definitely," remarked Sheridan. "Want to hear my reasons?"

"By all means," said Furillo.

150

Reliever Goose Gossage checked Dodgers in opening game.

Game 1	1	2	3	4	5	6	7	8	9	Total
Los Angeles	0	0	0	0	1	0	0	2	0	3
New York	3	0	1	1	0	0	0	0	x	5

"Let me start by saying that I feel the Dodgers will win it in six games," began Sheridan. "The fact that the Yanks swept Oakland isn't as convincing to me as the Dodgers coming from behind to beat Houston and Montreal. Oakland is a young team while both Houston and Montreal are veteran clubs. In fact, bouncing back to beat the Expos was quite an accomplishment. Montreal has the best home record in baseball.

"That is a factual analysis. There are some intangibles that I considered in picking the Dodgers. It may sound trite, but there is a revenge motive working for Los Angeles. They were virtually embarrassed in 1977 and again in 1978 and want to make amends. Then, too, the Yankee owner takes something out of the team with his outbursts. It affects their concentration. Billy Martin could handle it but a lame duck manager like Bob Lemon can't. Add it all up, and it's the Dodgers in six."

The experts had given the edge to the Yankees in every position except one—first base—where they rated Garvey better than Bob Watson both at bat and in the field. While they ranked Russell and rookie Larry Milbourne, who was replacing an injured Bucky Dent, as even at shortstop, they gave the Yanks the advantage at every other spot: Willie Randolph over Lopes at second base, Nettles over Ron Cey at third base, Rick Cerone over Mike Scioscia as catcher, Dave Winfield over Dusty Baker in left field, Jerry Mumphrey over Pedro Guerrero in center field and Jackson over Monday in right field.

While the starting pitchers for both teams were considered equal, the experts gave a big edge to the Yankees in the bullpen. They practically looked upon Goose Gossage as unhittable and figured that Ron Davis was the best number two reliever in baseball. The Yankee starters were expected to be Ron Guidry, Tommy John, Dave Righetti and Rick Reuschel. Los Angeles was expected to counter with Jerry Reuss, Fernando Valenzuela, Burt Hooton and Bob Welch. Looking over the bench, the scouts also figured the Yankees had the advantage. They felt that Lou Piniella, Bobby Murcer and Oscar Gamble were better hitters than Reggie Smith, Jay Johnstone and Ken Landreaux.

The presence of three Yankee lefthanders didn't go unnoticed by Dusty Baker, who was hoping such a challenge would finally lift the Dodgers out of a hitting slump that bogged them down during the playoffs. He even smiled at the thought of left-handed pitching.

"Lefties can get you back in a groove," said Baker. "You get a different look. But we haven't seen that many this year."

Although the weather was clear and crisp with the temperature at 54°, it was much warmer than Montreal. If anything, the Dodger players were conditioned to the chilly night air of Yankee Stadium after their exposure to winter in Canada. No one complained about the cold. After two remarkable comebacks in the playoffs, enabling the Dodgers to reach the World Series, their adrenalin was flowing freely.

The 79th World Series was billed as a colossal confrontation—Hollywood against the Big Apple. It was all that. The Yankee-Dodger rivalry was perhaps the most colorful in the history of the World Series. It also provided television coverage in the two biggest markets in the country—New York and Los Angeles. The moguls at ABC were happy, indeed. Games 1, 2, 6 and 7 were scheduled for New York; games 3, 4 and 5 were listed for Los Angeles.

With his flair for theatrics, Yankee owner George Steinbrenner had anticipated using veteran actor James Cagney to throw out the traditional first ball to open the Series. The popular 82-year-old Cagney, who lives on a farm in upstate New York, is best remembered for his role in the movie, "Yankee Doodle Dandy." Steinbrenner thought the appearance of Cagney would be a natural. However, Commissioner Bowie Kuhn rejected Steinbrenner's request, citing a baseball rule that prohibited the use of politicians and actors for such an occasion. Steinbrenner grunted, went back to his bench and named the widely admired Joe DiMaggio, lionized as the Yankee Clipper, to do the honors.

Although he was able to swing a bat, Jackson was not in the starting lineup. Since he could not run without pain, he would have been a handicap to the Yankee defense in right field.

Ron Guidry was the winning pitcher of the first game with seven strong innings.

Jackson has never been known for his fielding. He admitted that he didn't have any problem swinging during batting practice. Since the designated hitter rule was not in effect this year, Jackson's role would be reduced to pinch-hitter. He was replaced in right field by Piniella.

There were no other major changes. As expected, Reuss carried the Dodger hopes while Guidry walked out to the mound to prepare for his first pitch of the game. Lasorda was hoping to split the two games in New York before returning to Los Angeles for the next three games. He felt confident that Reuss, the number two man on his pitching staff, could neutralize the Yankee power hitters, especially with Jackson sitting on the bench.

GAME ONE

The crowd roared with anticipation at Guidry's first pitch. In his customary lead-off spot, Lopes stepped in and looked straight at Guidry. On the fourth pitch of the game,

Dusty Baker hits a sacrifice play in eighth inning.

Lopes hit a wicked shot to the left of Nettles. The Yankee third baseman dove to the ground, gloved the ball, stood up and quickly fired to first to nip the speeding Lopes by half a step. The play brought back memories of Nettles' spectacular fielding in 1978. The Dodgers were retired less dramatically after that as Russell grounded routinely to Milbourne and Baker popped up to Randolph.

The first Yankee batter to challenge Reuss was Randolph. The Dodger lefty didn't have any trouble. He got Randolph to ground out to Lopes. Then, Mumphrey got the first hit of the Series when he grounded a single through the right side of the infield. As big Dave Winfield walked into the batter's box, the crowd cheered. Three pitches later, they moaned as Winfield struck out swinging for the second out. Piniella, who was hitting in Jackson's spot, quickly got them cheering again by lining a ground rule double down the right field foul line. Watson, who like Winfield was an ex-National Leaguer, stepped in.

Bearing down, Reuss got him in a hole with two quick strikes. With the count at 1–2, Reuss looked for the sign from catcher Steve Yeager. He delivered a high fastball that Watson drove into the right center field bleachers. Suddenly, the Yankees rocketed to a 3–0 lead! It almost rose to 4–0 when Nettles ended the inning by flying out deep to Monday.

Garvey tried to get the Dodgers going by opening the second inning with a single off Nettle's glove. However, Guidry stopped them cold. He got Cey to pop up and then struck out Guerrero and Monday. The Yankees went out orderly in their turn at bat as Reuss got both Cerone and Milbourne to ground out and Guidry to strike out.

In the Dodgers' third turn at bat, Guidry had the crowd going wild. First, he struck out Yeager. When he did the same to Reuss, it marked his fourth consecutive strike out. The spectators loved it. Lopes ended the Guidry madness by grounding out to shortstop. Reuss seemed in command when he got Randolph on a ground ball to start the third inning. It was the fourth straight batter he retired. Mumphrey broke the chain with his second hit. Winfield created some anxiety by driving a ball deep to left center field, which Baker was successful in catching on the run. With Piniella up, Mumphrey stole second base. Piniella didn't leave him there. He lined a sharp single to left field that sent Mumphrey home with the fourth Yankee run. It was the end for Reuss. Bob Castillo replaced him. After some anxious moments, when Piniella stole second and Watson walked on four pitches, Castillo finally ended the inning by getting Nettles to ground out.

The Dodger hitting drought continued in the fourth inning. Russell bounced out, and Baker managed to come through with a base hit. He didn't advance any further, though, as both Garvey and Cey flied out without incident. Meanwhile, the Yanks continued to threaten in the bottom of the inning. Cerone started it with a walk. Milbourne forced him at second and reached that base himself a few moments later when Guidry sacrificed. Then Castillo lost control. He walked both Randolph and Mumphrey to fill the bases, bringing up the dangerous Winfield. He walked him, too, to force in Cerone with the Yanks' fifth run. Dave Goltz, who was summoned from the bullpen, prevented any further embarrassment by getting Piniella to pop out.

Still, the Dodgers needed runs. Los Angeles began feebly in the fifth inning. Guerrero flied out and Monday grounded to Randolph who made a fine backhand play on a sharply hit ball. Just when it seemed that Guidry would have an easy inning, Yeager jumped on his first pitch and drilled it into the right field stands for the Dodgers' first run. Lasorda then sent up Steve Sax to bat for Goltz and get something going. But he was retired. Watson greeted relief pitcher Tom Niedenfuer with a single to start the Yankee fifth. He remained there as Niedenfuer disposed of Nettles, Cerone and Milbourne.

Randolph took a hit away from Lopes on a solid play behind second base to open the sixth inning. After Russell flied out, Baker worked Guidry for a walk. Garvey, trying to get the Dodgers back in the game with one big swing, struck out. Niedenfuer continued to hold the Yanks, taking care of Guidry, Randolph and Mumphrey to retire six batters in a row.

It was getting late. The Dodgers had only three innings left to break through Guidry. Cey tried when he sent a screaming liner past a leaping Nettles. Winfield quickly retrieved the rebound off the fence and threw a dart to Randolph, who, in one motion, grabbed the throw and tagged out the belly-sliding Cey. The play loomed even bigger when Guerrero walked. However, Monday struck out for the second time and Yeager flied out to end the inning. Niedenfuer kept the Yankee hitters off balance. For the second consecutive inning, he set them down in order, running his string to nine.

When the Dodgers came up in the eighth inning, Guidry was gone. Lemon didn't hesitate to bring in Ron Davis, his number two arm in the bullpen. Derrel Thomas was sent up to bat for Niedenfuer and drew a walk. A few moments later he advanced to second on Cerone's passed ball with Lopes at bat. Davis, who seemed wild, proceeded to walk Lopes on four pitches. The Dodger dugout came alive as Davis was replaced by Gossage. Playing the percentages, Lasorda instructed Johnstone to pinch-hit for Russell. Johnstone came through. He lined a single to right that scored Thomas with the Dodgers' second run as Lopes raced around to third base.

Suddenly, the Dodgers had the tying run at bat with their big hitters coming up. Baker was first. He hit a sacrifice fly to Piniella that scored Lopes and cut New York's margin to 5–3. Garvey was next. Working carefully, Gossage ran the count to 3–1. Garvey swung on the next offering and drilled a shot that appeared headed down the third base foul line. However, the amazing Nettles leaped off the ground and speared the wicked liner, backhanded. The Dodgers were numb. Nettles had deprived them of a certain double. It didn't matter that Cey forced Johnstone to end the inning. Nettles had already stopped them. It also didn't matter that the Yanks went down harmlessly in the eighth and the Dodgers did the same in their final turn at bat. Nettles' catch, which earned him a standing ovation when he came up to hit in the eighth, killed them.

Lasorda knew it. He was still distraught in the Dodger clubhouse, long after the game was over.

"What the hell does he do when we come to town?" snapped Lasorda. "Does he get up for us? Does he do this all the time? Again, he did it. I've seen it before. What is it? Deja vu? Nettles is amazing. I get sick to my stomach seeing him make those plays all the time. He must go to bed hoping and praying he can kill us with his glove. There's no telling how far we could have gone, except for that play. The ninth inning was terrible. Pedro and Rick never saw the pitches they struck out on. Gossage just blew us away, but we'll be back."

Cey tried to explain Nettles' success, having observed his play over the years.

"We use the word 'cheat,' but we don't mean it the way we do with pitchers who scuff up the ball and things like that," said Cey. "But Nettles leans just before every pitch to give himself a little advantage. He has tremendous reflexes and great timing."

Garvey has memories of Nettles, too. He also has class. He wasn't overly upset at being deprived of what would have been at least a double by the Yankee third baseman.

"I remember those plays Graig made in '78," remarked Garvey. "He was exceptional then, too. The whole Yankee defense was great tonight. If Nettles and the rest of the Yankees weren't able to make plays like that, they wouldn't deserve to be in the World Series. New York is a team we can respect; and believe me, we respect them more after tonight. But don't forget, we came back. We were within one hit of tying it. It's typical of the way we have been hitting. It will help us for tomorrow."

Tomorrow was, definitely, another day. . . .

GAME TWO

It was no surprise when Lasorda turned to Burt Hooton to pitch the second game. Hooton was 10–6 during the season and was the number three starter behind Valenzuela and Reuss. Lasorda was depending on the

veteran to stop the Yankees and give him the split he was looking for in the two game series. Hooton was fairly successful in his World Series appearances against the Yanks, having won and lost one game each in both 1977 and 1978. The only lineup change Lasorda made was to start Ken Landreaux in centerfield, move Guerrero to right and Monday to the bench. Lasorda spoke positively before the game.

"How does it feel to be down 0–1?" He repeated a question directed at him. "Heck, we were down 0–2 in a five game series and won it. We are only down one game in a best-of-seven series. All it means is we lost the first game. But we've been in worse spots before in both playoffs that got us here. If we go out of here with a split, I'll be happy."

Hooton's mission wasn't easy. His adversary, Tommy John, was no stranger to the Dodgers. Far from it. In the 1978 Series with New York, John was the Dodger who pitched and lost against the Yankees. John had been a Dodger for six years and won 87 games for them despite an arm injury that almost ended his career.

Since he moved over to the Yankees, the 38-year-old John, who is known as the man with the bionic arm, has won 52 more times. Facing his ex-teammates for the first time, John was not caught up in a swell of emotion. He had both feet on the ground.

"It's going to be fun pitching against all my friends," said John. "If this had been the first year after I left, my emotions might be different. But there have been too many games since then to be wrapped up in what happened three or four years ago. It's an important game for us and for me, but only because it's the World Series. Besides, if I go out there thinking about getting back at the Dodgers. I'm going to over-pitch. I'm not going to be able to do my job. It really comes down to the fact that I'm not that type of person.

"I've had a lot of fun here and the park has been particularly good for me. It has a way of making up for a lot of high sinkers. I don't fear any of the Dodgers in this park, but I fear all of them in theirs. The Dodgers have a veteran team that's been here three times in

Tommy John faced his ex-teammates in second game.

Game 2	1	2	3	4	5	6	7	8	9	Total
Los Angeles	0	0	0	0	0	0	0	0	0	0
New York	0	0	0	0	1	0	0	2	x	3

the last seven years and gets better with age. If Bowie Kuhn would let me bet, I would have made a lot of money betting on the Dodgers when they were two games down to Houston and one down to the Expos. They know how to play in the clutch. Their experience is invaluable. The Dodgers are a lot like us in that way."

After Jimmy Cagney finally got to threw out the first ball, John walked calmly to the mound to see how much fun it would be for him. It was almost Los Angeles weather. The thermometer stood at 61 degrees; and since there wasn't any appreciable wind, it was considered warm for this time of year in New York. It was a great night for old friends to get together. In case any of them had forgotten him, John showed his ex-teammates his sinker. He quickly turned back Lopes, Russell and Baker to start the game.

Hooton was efficient. He opened the Yanks' half of the inning by walking Mumphrey. After two ground ball force-outs at second base, he walked Oscar Gamble who replaced Piniella in right field. With the troublesome Nettles at bat, Hooton slipped a third strike past him to get safely out of the inning. The way John looked in the first inning, it would have severely hindered the Dodgers if Nettles had gotten a hit and Los Angeles had fallen behind. When John's sinker is working, it is extremely difficult to catch up.

The Dodgers couldn't do anything with John in the second inning. Garvey grounded out to Nettles and Cey did the same. Guerrero didn't get the ball out of the infield either, bouncing out to Milbourne to end the inning. Then, for the second straight time, the Yankees got the first batter on base. Watson opened the second with a single, but Hooton hung tough. He got Cerone to fly to Guerrero and induced Randolph to force Watson at second. John made the third out by grounding to Lopes.

Facing the bottom of the Dodger batting order in the third, John continued to pitch flawlessly. Both Yeager and Landreaux grounded out. Hooton then struck out to become the ninth straight batter retired by John. However, Hooton answered back by setting down the Yankees in order for the first

time. He got Mumphrey and Milbourne on fly balls and Winfield on a grounder.

Still, the Dodgers couldn't solve John's pitches. In what appeared to be a replay of the first three innings, John continued to spin his magic. The pattern was the same. Lopes grounded out and so did Russell. Baker closed the inning by striking out. Hooton also continued to be effective. Although he was touched for a single by Nettles after Gamble flied out, he didn't waver. He got Watson to force Nettles and Cerone, in turn, to force Watson.

Purists who savor an old-fashioned pitching duel had one here. John was working on a perfect game, retiring all 12 batters he faced. Remarkably, only one ball by Lopes, who led off the game, reached the outfield. Two of the Dodgers were strike-out victims. The remaining nine were frustrated by ground balls. That's the way it is when John's sinker is working. On the other hand, Hooton had allowed only two base hits and issued two walks, leaving the only four runners in the scoreless struggle stranded.

Starting off the fifth inning, Garvey abruptly dispelled any thoughts of a perfect game by grounding a single over second base for the Dodgers' first hit. Cey then topped a ball to Nettles, whose only play was to throw the slow-footed batter out at first while Garvey advanced to second base. Guerrero hit another ground ball. Milbourne bobbled it, however, and suddenly there were Dodger runners on third and first with only one out.

Lasorda clapped his hands in the dugout. He fully expected his club would break through with at least a run. The way the game was progressing, one run was big enough. Landreaux had the opportunity to put the Dodgers ahead. Instead, John met the challenge and recorded a big strike-out. Now it was up to Yeager. He hit a bullet that appeared to be headed for center field. Instinctively, John threw up his glove at the white blur that whizzed by his ear, interrupting its flight. It fell to the ground, and he quickly grabbed it and threw to Watson. The throw wasn't all that accurate, pulling Watson off the base. Watson succeeded in one-handing the toss and tagging Yeager as he

Davey Lopes takes late throw as Larry Milbourne slides safely into second base with a double.

Steve Yeager is out on close play after colliding with Yankee first baseman Bob Watson.

crashed into him. It was the game's biggest play and prevented the Dodgers from scoring. John and Yeager smiled at one another as they returned to their dugouts.

The Yankees got a break when they got up. Randolph reached first base when Lopes misplayed his ground ball. As expected, John sacrificed him to second. It appeared that Hooton would get out of the inning after Mumphrey flied out to Landreaux. However, with two out, Milbourne lined a double down the left field line, bringing Randolph in with the first run of the night. Hooton squelched any further scoring by getting Winfield on a bouncer to Lopes.

The question now as the Dodgers came up in the sixth inning was whether or not the one run was all that was needed. Lasorda let Hooton bat and he struck out. Lopes was thrown out by Nettles for the second out.

Russell then hit a smash that Nettles dove for but couldn't stop from going into left field for a single. Nettles then recorded his third assist of the inning when he fielded Baker's roller and forced Russell at second. Hooton kept the Yanks off base by getting Gamble and Nettles on fly balls and Watson on a grounder to Russell.

Once more Garvey tried to get the Dodgers going. He opened the seventh with his second straight hit, a single to left. Cey almost put the Dodgers ahead but Gamble hauled in his fly ball in deep right field. Guerrero hit the ball hard, but Milbourne speared his line drive for the second out. Landreaux ended the mild threat with a fly ball to Winfield. When the Yankees came to bat, Hooton suddenly lost his control. He walked both Cerone and Randolph at the start of the inning. Seeking to break the game open, Lemon sent Bobby

160

Murcer up to bat for John. Lasorda then made his move. He brought in Terry Forster to face Murcer, a lefthanded hitter who immediately sacrificed both runners. With first base open, Lasorda ordered Forster to walk Mumphrey. A moment later the strategy paid off as Milbourne grounded into a double play that was started by Russell.

The Dodgers still needed runs. The appearance of Gossage on the mound didn't increase their chances. Johnstone, pinch-hitting for Yeager, brought the crowd to its feet by flying deep to Gamble. Smith, batting for Forster, got a broken bat single to right. Monday then batted for Lopes, as Lasorda was thinking "home run." Monday struck out, swinging, and Russell popppped up to end the inning as Steve Howe came in to pitch. After disposing of Winfield, Howe ran into trouble. Piniella hit for Gamble and lined a single to center. When Nettles looped a single to the same spot, Dave Stewart replaced Howe. Watson promptly singled to score Bobby Brown, who had run for Piniella, with the Yanks' second run. Stewart then threw wildly on an attempted pick-off play at second base as the runners moved around to second and third. Cerone was purposely walked to load the bases. The Los Angeles infield set up for an inning-ending double play. However, Randolph drove a ball deep to Guerrero for a sacrifice fly that gave the Yankees a 3–0 lead. It didn't matter that Gossage struck out to complete the inning.

Facing Gossage in the ninth inning was no enviable task. After Baker grounded out, Garvey got on base for the third time by walking on a 3–2 pitch. Gossage then reared back and struck out both Cey and Guerrero. The Dodgers, their hopes for a split dashed, had lost the first two games. The guarded talk of a Yankee sweep filled the New York clubhouse. After all, only seven teams in the history of the World Series had ever come back and won it all.

"Sweep?" said Lasorda, who seemed upset at the thought. "My rear end, that's what they'll sweep. It isn't that we're not hitting, it's just that they are pitching. It was a tough loss for us. It makes our job even harder now. We were really hoping for a split here. We were

down in a best-of-five series against Houston and Montreal and won. Now we're down in a best-of-seven series. I think any time you're down 2–0 it's tough to come back. But we have confidence we can do it. I want to leave you with these words of wisdom: Baseball is like driving; it's the one who gets home safely that counts."

The players weren't distraught to the point of swearing and throwing things. Rather, they kept things in perspective.

"They've gotten the breaks," Cey pointed out. "We've had our backs to the wall before. The character of this club has been tested from day one of post-season play. I think we can do it again. We've been one hit away in each of the games here. Things are bound to turn around sooner or later."

What the Dodgers needed was some hitting. Actually Lasorda felt Hooton pitched a fine game, good enough to win. Surprisingly, Hooton didn't think so.

"I felt good, but I just didn't have any zip on the ball," he disclosed. "It might have looked to everyone else that I pitched well, but I lost it in about the third or fourth inning. I made a few bad pitches they didn't hit. But the bad one to Milbourne is the one that beat me."

It had just happened to be John's night. He'd allowed only three hits and three fly balls in the seven innings he pitched. Yet, John was stoic about his performance.

"The game had no special meaning other than it was a World Series game," said John. "People were asking me all week if it was a big advantage for me to be pitching against a team I had played for. Sometimes knowledge is a dangerous thing. You tend to get off your normal game. I pitched tonight like I was pitching against the Cincinnati Reds or the Milwaukee Brewers. I had to put everything out of my mind and pitch my game. I had to say, 'Hey, these are batters up there, major league hitters. Good ones!' I couldn't say to myself this is Garvey, Cey, Dusty, and Yeager, and Russell and Lopes. I had my job to do. My satisfaction is being in a World Series and winning it. Hey, these guys on the Dodgers are my friends. We shared a lot of memories together."

The Dodgers were going home for the

weekend together, hoping to find the batting shoes they'd left behind. . . .

GAME THREE

On Thursday the Dodgers welcomed a day off. They had scored only three runs in the two games in New York but were even more concerned about their slumbering bats. Their protracted hitting slump went back even further, to the very start of the post season playoffs. In the 12 games, they had scored only 31 runs with a feeble team batting average of .204. In their six losses they were shut out three times and managed to score only one run on two occasions and three runs another—hardly figures upon which championships are built.

In the warmth of Dodger Stadium, Reggie Smith was giving it a try in the outfield. Ever since he had major surgery on his throwing shoulder a year ago, Smith hadn't been able to throw a ball hard enough or long enough. Sidelined throughout most of the regular season, Smith made only two appearances on the field, both times at first base. The Dodgers sorely missed his bat. The loss was heightened by their pallid hitting in recent weeks. If anyone yearned for the designated hitter innovation, it was Smith.

"Obviously we need some offense," said Smith. "I don't know if I can do it, but I'd sure like to try."

His chances seemed slim. He realized it, too.

"Winning is winning," said Smith. "And I still think we're going to win this thing. I don't know how but maybe playing me will help do it. If I don't get the chance, I won't be terribly disappointed. Just disappointed. There's a difference."

Smith played catch in the outfield with a batting practice pitcher to see if there was any difference in his arm. He lobbed a ball back and forth several times. He really couldn't cut loose. His arm betrayed him again. Smith made it known that he couldn't play in the outfield.

The absence of one Yankee player this time caused the Dodgers to be downright joyful. Nettles, who was like a vacuum cleaner at third base, was nursing a painfully swollen right thumb. During the sixth inning of Wednesday night's game, he jammed his thumb while diving for Russell's base hit. Although the thumb bothered him, he continued in the game and even singled his last time at bat in the eight inning. He didn't tell anybody about the injury until after the game. Still, he figured a day's rest would be all that was needed. He was wrong. On Thursday the swelling on his thumb was deemed bad enough to require a splint.

"I was just hoping that it wouldn't swell up," said Nettles who lives in nearby San Diego "When I fell on my hand I knew almost immediately I hurt it. I just didn't know how bad. Right now it's very swollen and very sore, and I won't go out there if the chance exists that I'll hurt the club. I'm a fast healer, and I'm optimistic. I'm very disappointed since my family was coming up from San Diego for the games here."

It was not known if the Yankees' other celebrated absentee, Reggie Jackson, would play. He tested his pulled calf muscle in the outfield and took his normal turn in the batting cage. The Yankees won the first two games without him, so there was no need to panic about his condition, at least not for the time being.

"I think I can play," said Jackson. "The weather is warmer and the outfield is softer. If we were down two games, I'd definitely force myself to play. The way it is, guys like Piniella and Watson have been carrying us and I'm more appreciative than frustrated."

The drama surrounding the third game was as high as it had been for the opener. Two of the most exciting rookie pitchers in baseball memory created the charged atmosphere. Playing every angle, the Dodgers had wisely dispatched their valuable parcel of Mexican gold, Fernando Valenzuela, on a plane a day ahead of the team to provide him with an extra 24 hours of rest.

While Valenzuela had been burning National League baseball trails during the early part of the season with his shutouts and strikeouts, the Yankee rookie sensation, Dave Rigetti, who was opposing Valenzuela, had been toiling in the minor league with Columbus. After he was called up, the 22-year-old Righetti finished with an 8–4

Fernando Valenzuela carried Dodger hopes in third game.

Game 3										
	1	2	3	4	5	6	7	8	9	Total
New York	0	2	2	0	0	0	0	0	0	4
Los Angeles	3	0	0	0	2	0	0	0	x	5

record and an ERA of 2.05. He was even more impressive in the championship playoffs where he was 3–0 with a 0.60 ERA, having struck out 17, allowing only one run and 12 hits in 15 innings.

The match-up of the two stellar rookies was looked upon as the stuff of which dreams are made. Like Valenzuela, Righetti was a left-hander. It was the first match-up of rookies in the World Series since 1967 when Dick Highes of the St. Louis Cardinals opposed Gary Waslewski of the Boston Red Sox. Historians will also tell you that it was only the third time rookie pitchers have started against each other in something as big as the World Series.

On the morning of the game, an earthquake in the early hours aroused the Yankee players from their sleep. Local sportscasters made light of it, remarking that maybe the quake would wake up the Dodgers' hitters instead. By evening, though, everything was calm. Jackson wasn't in the lineup for the third straight game. Perhaps the thought of Valenzuela's pitching influenced Lemon's decision to rest him another day.

The weather was a warm 73 degrees as Dodger great, Sandy Koufax, threw out the ceremonial first ball. Valenzuela and the rest of the Dodgers knew they were home after spending almost a week in chilling temperatures. This game was monumental for Los Angeles. No team, having lost the first two games, had ever won the World Series. The Dodgers were in a mood to attempt to become the first. They were confident they had a stopper in Valenzuela.

The anticipation of the Dodger rookie's first pitch created a stir among the record 56,236 partisans. Randolph looked over Valenzuela's pitches and extracted a walk on a 3–2 pitch. Mumphrey forced Randolph but Winfield walked on four pitches. Valenzuela didn't appear as sharp as he normally does. However, he laid to rest any fears of a big inning by inducing Piniella to crack into a double play as the big crowd cheered

Lopes, who worked Righetti to a full count, smacked a double down the right field foul line to open the Dodger inning. Russell kept the fans cheering by beating out a bunt as Lopes took third. The Dodgers had their

biggest threat of the Series going. However, in anxiety, Baker popped up. The crowd then moaned when Garvey struck out. Were the Dodgers going to be denied again?

It was all up to Cey. The count had reached 2–1. Righetti tried to throw one past Cey. The Dodger slugger caught hold of the fastball but drove it foul well back into the left field seats. Desperation lined his face. Cey coiled his arms again, waiting for the next pitch. Again, Righetti tested him with a fast one. Once more Cey made good contact and delivered the ball loudly over a helpless Dave Winfield for a three-run homer. Dodger joy was rampant. It was as if they'd won the Series. The frustrations of the first two games were wiped clean with one swing of Cey's bat. The Dodgers led for the first time. After Guerrero was hit by a pitch and Monday beat out an infield hit, it looked as if they might score again. But Yeager popped out to end the delirious inning.

Giving Valenzuela a three-run lead was like handing out food stamps in Beverly Hills. It was unheard of. Watson didn't know anything about that though and hit his second home run to start the Yankees' second inning. Neither did Cerone. He just missed a homer by smashing a double off the left field fence. Aurelio Rodriguez, who replaced Nettles in the lineup, flied deep enough to Monday to advance Cerone to third. He scored the Yanks' second run a moment later when Milbourne singled to right. A few arms began to loosen in the Dodger bullpen. After Righetti sacrificed, Randolph worked Valenzuela for his second walk. The tension broke when Mumphrey grounded out to end the uprising.

The crowd's sentiments were with Valenzuela when he came up to bat. They applauded even more when he drew a walk. Lopes bunted him to second. He moved to third on Russell's ground ball but remained there as Baker popped out for the second time.

Winfield was Valenzuela's first strike out, opening the third inning. Piniella singled to center for the Yankees' fourth hit. Cerone then took Valenzuela's first pitch for a ball. On the next one he belted it to the same spot where he doubled, only this time the ball

Aurelio Rodriguez couldn't stop Bill Russell's fourth inning single.

carried further. It landed in the left center field stands for a home run that gave the Yankees a 4–3 lead. Dodger fans were stunned, and they grew restless when Rodriguez out-legged an infield bouncer and Milbourne was walked intentionally. Righetti eased their fear, however, by striking out.

Garvey became the Dodgers' potential tying run when he initiated the third inning with a single. Righetti, pitching cautiously to Cey, walked him. Lemon had had enough. He replaced Righetti with George Frazier, who immediately struck out Guerrero. Monday flied to Winfield for the second out. Lasorda went to his bench and sent up the lefthand-hitter, Scioscia, to bat for Yeager. Frazier got out of the inning by getting Scioscia on a grounder.

In the fourth, Valenzuela got Randolph and Mumphrey on ground balls to Russell but lost Winfield on a 3–2 pitch for his fifth walk of the contest. It didn't hurt him, as Piniella lined to Baker for the third out. Although the Dodger bullpen was ready, Lasorda let

Valenzuela bat in the bottom of the frame. He grounded out and so did Lopes. Russell slapped a single, but Baker forced him for the third out.

Watson kept the pressure on Valenzuela by doubling to begin the fifth inning. Cerone, who had doubled and homered, stepped in. Valenzuela reared back and struck him out as he swung. Watson moved to third on Rodriguez' grounder to Lopes. After Milbourne was intentionally walked for the second straight time, Valenzuela struck out Frazier to retire the Yankees.

Leading off for the second inning in a row, Garvey chopped a single behind third. Again, Cey walked just as he had done in the third inning. Guerrero, who hadn't gotten a hit in eight times at bat, finally broke through. He bounced a double over Rodriguez's head that scored Garvey with the tying run. Now the Dodgers had runners on third and second with none out. Monday was walked intentionally to load the bases. Lemon then made his second pitching change by bringing in

166

lefthander Rudy May to face Scioscia. The strategy worked—but for the Dodgers. Scioscia grounded into a double play as Cey scored to put the Dodgers back in front, 5–4. It didn't matter that Valenzuela grounded out to end the inning. He had a one-run lead to protect.

The pesky Randolph opened the sixth inning by walking for the third time. He tested Scioscia's arm and was thrown out, stealing. Valenzuela then struck out Mumphrey and got Winfield on a bouncer to Cey. Lopes started the Dodgers off with a single but Russell flied out, Baker fanned and Garvey popped out to leave him stranded.

In the Yankees' seventh, Valenzuela had his easiest inning of the contest. He retired the Yanks in orderly fashion for the first time, getting Piniella and Watson on outfield flies and Cerone on a pop up. Looking for an insurance run, Cey opened the Los Angeles half of the inning with a base hit. However, Guerrero struck out and Derrel Thomas, batting for Monday, grounded into an inning-ending double play.

The excitement began to build for the final two innings. Could Valenzuela hold a one-run lead to provide the Dodgers with their first victory? There were some anxious moments when Rodriguez opened the eighth with a single and Milbourne scratched a hit off Lopes' glove. The Yankees were seriously threatening. Murcer batted for May and tried to bunt. An alert Cey charged in and caught his pop while diving across the foul line. He instantly got to his feet and threw to Garvey to double Milbourne off first. Cey completed the inning by grabbing Randolph's bouncer and tagging the approaching Rodriguez. Dodger fans were no longer apprehensive.

It was of no consequence that the Dodgers wasted a lead-off single by Scioscia at the beginning of the eighth inning. Although the Dodgers would have been grateful for another run off the Yanks' new reliever, Ron Davis, they realized the final outcome depended on Valenzuela's arm. The Mexican received a generous ovation when he came up to hit. He tried to move Scioscia over to second but ended up forcing him instead. The faithful could have cared less that Lopes fanned and

Russell popped up. They were waiting to see Valenzuela overpower the Yankees in their final at-bat.

Mumphrey was up first and grounded out to Lopes. Winfield was next. He was due. He had not gotten a hit in nine tries. Valenzuela made it ten by getting him to fly out to Guerrero. All that remained was Piniella. The throng roared with every pitch. Valenzuela was one strike away from giving Los Angeles its much-needed win. Valenzuela threw. The crowd stood and cheered as Piniella swung and missed. It was a thrilling finale. The kid actor had stolen the show.

It was a gutsy exhibition by a youngster. He was raked for nine hits, including two home runs, and seven walks, leaving nine runners on base. It wasn't vintage Valenzuela. Instead, he was like a champion boxer who keeps getting staggered but comes back until he wins. He threw an abnormally high number (145) of pitches but was at his best at the end when it was up to him to win or lose.

Lasorda was the first to acknowledge Valenzuela's achievement. His delight was obvious.

"I told the team after the game that Fernando gave one of the gutsiest performances I've ever seen for a young man," beamed Lasorda. "He didn't have his good stuff, that was apparent. I came close to removing him several times. He was like a poker player out there, bluffing his way through some bad hands. But did you see him when he smelled that one-run lead? I've said it before, but tonight he showed again he's one of the toughest closers in the business, the toughest I've seen in many, many years."

Lasorda himself displayed enough guts in sticking with the rookie lefthander. He, too, was gambling like a champion poker player on what he called "the year of Fernando."

"We knew from the start that Fernando didn't have his best stuff," admitted Lopes. "It was a courageous thing on Lasorda's part to stick with Fernando. If we'd lost, Tommy would have been subject to a lot of criticism."

Scioscia, who was closest to Valenzuela from the fourth inning on, saw the difference in his pitching.

"When I caught him, everything was down,"

he explained. "When I was watching him from the bullpen, everything looked high. It's just that when Fernando gets tired, he gets into the game. Once the adrenalin runs out, he's able to threw more smoothly and to stay down with his screwball and slider."

The emotion over Valenzuela's win almost drowned out acclaim for Cey's heroic contributions to the game. He not only produced a loud, three-run homer in the first inning, but he turned in a rally-ending double play with a circus catch in the eighth frame. But he seems used to being in the background.

"I've never gone into a World Series where the writers hadn't given the other team the edge at third base," Cey said. "That can't bother me. Opinion is one thing; what I've done is another."

Later, after the excitement had died down someone asked Valenzuela what he thought about the earthquake that shook Los Angeles in the morning. Valenzuela, who doesn't speak English, answered through an interpreter.

"I thought the earthquake was tonight, they were hitting the ball so hard," he quipped.

GAME FOUR

The fact that Valenzuela stopped the Yankees on an off night, and prevented a sweep, rankled Steinbrenner. The Yankee owner made an appearance in the clubhouse after the game to make his feelings known. He had done that on several occasions during the season so it came as no surprise to the players. This time, instead of screaming and shouting, Steinbrenner reserved his criticism for Lemon. Still, though he got some things off his chest, one could sense that Mr. Steinbrenner was about to erupt.

"You let a team like the Dodgers up and you've made a foolish mistake," he snapped.

What Steinbrenner wanted was to be assured that Jackson would be returned to the lineup in Game 4, having missed the first three. If Lemon had been uncertain about starting him, Steinbrenner made sure that he would. The fact that Mumphrey and Winfield, the team's second and third hitters, were not producing was also disturbing Steinbrenner. Mumphrey had gotten only two hits in ten

at-bats. Winfield was still looking for his first. Steinbrenner wanted changes.

By the next afternoon they were made. On a warm, sunny afternoon, the first daytime game of the Series attracted another record crowd to Dodger Stadium. The attendance figure of 56,242 was better, by six people, than the record set the night before.

The Yankees had a new look in their outfield. Jackson, a familiar figure to Dodger fans in the 1977 and 1978 Series, was back at his old spot in right field. However, Oscar Gamble was in leftfield instead of Winfield. Winfield wasn't benched. Rather, he was moved over to center field while Mumphrey was given a seat in the dugout.

Lasorda named righthander Bob Welch to oppose Yankee righthander Rick Reuschel. The veteran Reuschel wasn't a stranger to the Dodgers, having pitched for the Chicago Cubs since 1972 before he was acquired by the Yankees in June. In starting Welch, Lasorda was taking something of a gamble. Welch had not started a game for three weeks. Lasorda's thinking was that if he could get by with Welch, he would have his regular rotation of Reuss, Hooton and Valenzuela working with an extra day's rest.

Second-guessers were vocal before the first inning was even over. Randolph, going to right field, lined a ball and wound up on third base with a triple. Milbourne hit a shot in almost the same spot for a double. Then, before fans could digest a hot dog, the Yankees had a run on two hard-hit balls. The hitless Winfield settled for a walk, which set the stage for Jackson's first appearance. Memories of '77 and '78 were stirred as the Yanks' gifted October slugger measured his stance at home plate. Jackson didn't disappoint the crowd. He smashed a hard single to left and loaded the bases.

The Yankees were on the verge of a big inning. Lasorda realized it and took out Welch, replacing him with Dave Goltz. Welch's departure came earlier than any starter in the past 17 years. He had faced just four batters and thrown only 16 pitches. Goltz brought a moment of relief when Gamble's fly to Guerrero was too shallow to permit Milbourne to tag from third. Now the Dodgers were

Ron Cey tags out Yankees' Willie Randolph.

Game 4	1	2	3	4	5	6	7	8	9	Total
New York	2	1	1	0	0	2	0	1	0	7
Los Angeles	0	0	2	0	1	3	2	0	x	8

Steve Garvey missed tagging out Willie Randolph on a close pick-off play.

thinking "double play" with the slow-footed Watson. They didn't get it. Watson flied deep enough to Baker to allow Milbourne to score the Yanks' second run. Cerone ended the excitement by forcing Jackson at second.

The score could have been a lot worse when the Dodgers came to bat. Most teams would be happy to have one run in a bases-loaded situation and with none out. The 2–0 deficit wasn't that big. After Lopes and Russell both bounced out to third, Garvey slapped a single to right. Cey, who had belted a three-run homer in the first inning the night before, came up thinking "long ball" again. He tried, but lined to Winfield instead.

When it appeared that Goltz would have an easy inning in the second, the Dodgers fell even further behind. Goltz fanned Rodriguez

and Reuschel. However, Randolph, who is not known for his home runs, cracked one over the fence in right center field for a 3–0 lead before Milbourne ended the inning by grounding out. The Dodgers hit Reuschel hard but they couldn't do anything. After both Baker and Monday lined out, Guerrero dropped a single to center. Scioscia then hit another line drive that Gamble pulled down in left field.

After leading off in the fourth inning, Winfield still couldn't get his first hit. However, Jackson got his second on a grounder up the middle. Gamble forced Jackson for the second out but Watson walked to bring up Cerone. The Yankee catcher unleashed a single through the left side to score Gamble and push the Yankees' advantage to 4–0. A short time later the bases were loaded when Rodriguez beat out a bouncer to deep short. A hit now would put the game out of reach. Fortunately, Reuschel came up and forced Rodriguez at second, to end the inning.

Still, the Dodgers were behind, 4–0. They had to get back in the game quickly. Landreaux came through as a pinch-hitter for Goltz by grounding a double past first base. Lopes didn't wait long to score him by lining a single to right. Then he showed the Yankees his speed by stealing second. After Russell was called out on strikes, Garvey beat out a slow roller to Rodriguez and Lopes went to third. Cey came up, representing what could have been the tying run, but overswung and topped a ball to Milbourne. It allowed Lopes to score and Garvey to take second, but Baker, fighting a slump, struck out to kill the rally.

As Forster entered the game in the fourth inning the Dodgers had made up half of the runs needed to tie the game. He walked Randolph, who was promptly sacrificed to second by Milbourne. Winfield bounced to short and Randolph tried to make it to third but was cut down on Russell's throw to Cey. Jackson then worked Forster for a walk as Gamble came up. Lopes made a fine stop on his grounder to prevent the ball from going into right field. Instead of another run, the Yankees had the bases loaded again. Forster met the challenge and got Watson to force Gamble without any further damage.

Los Angeles had a fine opportunity to score in their turn at bat but failed. Monday opened the fourth with a walk and reached second when Guerrero grounded a single past Milbourne. At that point Lemon went to the mound and relieved Reuschel with May. Scioscia sacrificed both runners into scoring position. Lasorda sent up Smith to bat for Forster, anticipating a hit that would tie the game 4–4. But Smith struck out, swinging on three pitches, and Lopes grounded out to the dismay of Dodger fans.

Niedenfuer came on to pitch the fifth inning and had no trouble retiring Cerone, Rodriguez and May in order. The Dodgers needed some runs. After Russell flied out, Garvey ripped a double down the left field line. Cey followed with a single to left that scored Garvey with the Dodgers' third run. That was enough for Forster; Lemon replaced him with hard-throwing Ron Davis. Firing with precision, Davis struck out Baker and Monday to leave Los Angeles short.

Russell misplayed Randolph's grounder to open the sixth inning, then Milbourne fouled out and Winfield flied deep to Baker, enabling Randolph to move up a base. With first base open, Lasorda ordered Jackson to be walked, taking his chances with Gamble instead. However, Gamble lashed a single to right that scored Randolph and sent Jackson to third base. Watson then hit a sinking liner to left. Baker dove for it and, for an instant, appeared to have caught it. Left field umpire Nick Colosi ruled that Baker had merely trapped it and Jackson tallied the Yanks' sixth run Cerone flied to Monday for the final out of the inning.

Brown, who ran for Gamble, stayed in the game in center field as Winfield moved over to left. Down 6–3, the Dodgers needed a spark. Guerrero flied out, but Scioscia walked. Then Jay Johnstone picked out a bat and went up to hit for Niedenfuer. He caught hold of Davis' fastball and delivered it into the right center field stands for a home run. The two-run blast ignited the Dodgers. Lopes hit a fly ball to Jackson, who had trouble catching it. The ball bounced off Jackson's chest for a two-base error as Lopes raced to second. He kept the pressure on by stealing third, his second stolen base of the game. Russell then singled to center, deadlocking the contest at 6–6. Chagrined, Lemon sent Davis to the showers and called on George Frazier to put out the fire. Frazier did so by getting Garvey and Cey to fly to Winfield.

Dodger fans were mildly ecstatic. The game was just tied, but an inning before Los Angeles had been three runs behind. Steve Howe was brought in to keep the Yanks in check in the seventh inning. He was greeted with a single by Rodriguez who tried to stretch it into a double but was put out on Guerrero's strong throw to Russell. Howe then turned back Frazier and Randolph on easy outs.

The momentum of the game had changed. It was obvious when Baker beat out a slow roller to short and Monday followed with a bloop double that was misplayed by Brown. The Dodgers were in an excellent position to take the lead for the first time in the game. After Guerrero was walked intentionally, Lemon made still another pitching change, his fourth of the game. He surprised everyone by calling for Tommy John. He was banking on John's sinker to keep the ball in the infield. Yeager, batting for Scioscia, didn't give him a chance. He lifted a sacrifice fly ball to Jackson that scored Baker with the go-ahead run. Howe then did his job and bunted both runners along. Lopes gave the Dodgers an insurance run when he beat out a high chopper to third that scored Monday. Russell finally brought the wildly impossible inning to a close by grounding out to Milbourne.

It was up to Howe to preserve an 8–6 lead as the Dodgers took the field in the eighth inning with some lineup changes. Yeager remained in the game to catch while Guerrero moved back to right field, allowing Derrel Thomas to take over in center. Thomas immediately got some action. He grabbed

Milbourne's liner and then ran back to pull down Winfield's long drive. But he couldn't do anything about Jackson's blast. The Dodger nemesis unloaded a home run over the right center field wall that trimmed the Dodgers' lead to 8–7. Now there was concern. Howe eased the tension for the moment by throwing out Piniella, who batted for Gamble, on a one hopper back to the mound.

It would relieve the strain if the Dodgers could pick up a run in their turn at bat. The way the game was going, a one-run lead wasn't exactly a lock. After Garvey struck out, Cey lined a sharp single to right. John kept him there by getting Baker on a fly and striking out Thomas to finish his day's work.

Los Angeles was only three outs away from deadlocking the Series at 2–2. Watson grounded out to Russell. Cerone kept Yankee hopes alive by bouncing a hit up the middle. Barry Foote was picked to pinch-hit for Rodriguez. Howe quickly disposed of him by striking him out on three pitches. There was only one out left. Murcer grabbed a bat to hit

Davey Lopes successfully steals second base in third inning.

for John. He bounced a grounder to Garvey who knocked the ball down and threw to Howe who was covering first base. When Howe misplayed the ball, Murcer was safe on the error. Tension mounted. A moment later it erupted into cheers as Thomas caught Randolph's fly ball for the game-ending put-out. After three hours, 32 minutes and 36 players, the Dodgers got even by overpowering four- and three-run deficits against the best bullpen in baseball.

The Dodgers could barely contain their joy in the clubhouse. "I was sitting on the bench in the top of the inning and watching everything go wrong for us," said Johnstone, the reserve outfielder whose sixth inning home run had been the turning point in the game. "So when I got a chance to go up there, the home run was on my mind. It could change everything for us. In that situation, I know the pitcher is going to be throwing awfully hard, so I have to cut down on my swing. I was just looking for a fastball I could hit."

Howe had admittedly gotten away with murder. Although he allowed only three hits and a run in the three innings he worked, the only pitches that made him happy were those that the Yankee batters didn't hit.

"You want to talk about baffling them with bull?" exclaimed Howe. "My wife could have thrown better than I did. But I feel great about this. We're even now. It's a three-game playoff."

Lasorda takes it one game at a time. Otherwise the pressure would kill him.

"It was the most exciting game I've ever been involved in," he said. "I'm going to ask them to do it one more time, to battle back and win this Series. My legs are so rubbery and I'm so tired from cheering that I just want to go home and sleep."

There was still time. The players wanted to relish the win a little while longer.

"It wasn't your basic Picasso, but it's better to have a few smiles than not," said Monday. "It certainly means a lot to our ballclub to come back from two down. We have played better over the past two weeks when we've been behind. However, it certainly hasn't been by design. We really would have preferred to be in front."

GAME FIVE

Now, it was the Yankees who were pressured. The 78th World Series was deadlocked after four games and they were looking over their shoulders. In the last two games the Yanks left a total of 21 runners on base. That wasn't any way to win a world championship. Steinbrenner knew it; it was not his style. He was obsessed with winning, perhaps more so than any other owner in baseball. Before the decisive fifth game, Steinbrenner ordered the doors to the Yankee clubhouse closed while he spoke to the players. Though he had been appalled by the sloppy base running and the shoddy relief pitching in the last two games, he was calm during his dissertation. He told the players it would be the last time this year that he would talk to them.

"I'm through," said Steinbrenner later. "I've said all I'm going to say. They understand what they have to do. I don't think they want to be an embarrassment to New York. That's why I'm so cocky and sure we're going to win. But some guys are going to have to start doing it instead of talking about it. I reminded them that the Series had become a two-out-of-three affair, that they were going to get the Dodgers back in New York right where they wanted them. If I had planned the script, I wouldn't have written it any other way."

Lasorda and the Dodgers were busy writing their own script. Hooton and Valenzuela would be rested for Broadway, and Reuss would be ready for the pivotal fifth game. Although Reuss lasted less than three innings in the Series' opener, Lasorda felt confident that the veteran lefthander would bounce back with a powerful performance. He was convinced that the additional day of rest that he gained for Reuss, by starting Welch the day before, would benefit him.

Reuss would have to be good. He was once again matched against Guidry, the hardest thrower of all the Yankee starters. It has been the Yankees' strategy to let Guidry throw as hard as he can for six or seven innings and let either Gossage or Davis finish up. That was the pattern that evolved during the playoffs and it was maintained in the opening game in

New York. Guidry's fastball blazed for seven innings. Then he yielded only four hits, struck out seven and earned a victory while Gossage collected the last six outs.

On Sunday the temperature was 75, three degrees higher than the day before. It was sunny and there still wasn't any wind to worry about. There were fewer people in the stands, too. A crowd of 56,115 turned out for the game. Lasorda had made one lineup change. He gave Derrel Thomas, a switch hitter, his first start in center field and inserted him in the eighth spot in the batting order. Since Guidry was lefthanded, Yeager was behind the plate instead of Scioscia.

Reuss had no difficulty in the opening inning. He got both Randolph and Milbourne on grounders, then had the crowd cheering by striking out Winfield for the third out. Guidry struck out Lopes to start things off, and got Russell on a pop to Rodriguez. Garvey continued his hot hitting with a bloop single to center and Guidry lost Cey on a 3–2 pitch. The Dodgers had runners on first and second but Baker lined out to Piniella to end the inning.

Jackson continued to scour Dodger pitching. He opened the second inning with a double, his fourth hit in as many times at bat. When Lopes booted Watson's ground ball, the Yankees had runners on third and first with none out. Piniella followed with a single that scored Jackson as Watson stopped at second. It appeared as though the Yankees were going to break the game open. Reuss stood on the mound with his hands on his hips. He took a deep breath and concentrated on Cerone. Cerone hit a slider on the ground that Russell turned into a double play. Rodriguez left Watson stranded on third. Reuss had gotten out of trouble.

After Guerrero flied deep to Winfield, the Dodgers wasted an opportunity to score. Yeager followed with a double off the left center field fence. However, he remained there as Thomas flied out and Reuss was called out on strikes.

Reuss ran into more trouble in the third inning. He started out all right by fanning Guidry. However, when Randolph walked and

Milbourne hit safely to left field, the Yankees again looked threatening. Winfield was denied for the fifteenth time as he forced Milbourne at second with Randolph moving to third. Jackson's appearance had the crowd buzzing. Reuss went with his best against the dangerous slugger and struck him out swinging. Still, the Dodgers couldn't solve Guidry. He set down Lopes on a fly, Russell on a grounder and Garvey on strikes.

Reuss couldn't avoid danger. He walked Watson on four pitches to open the fourth frame. Piniella then bounced to Lopes on a play the Dodger second baseman would like to forget. First he bobbled the ball for one error, then he threw it into the Yankee dugout for another, as Watson advanced to third base and Piniella to second. It looked as if the Yankees would score this time. With the infield in, Cerone grounded to Russell. Watson held third as Cerone was thrown out. Lasorda instructed Reuss to walk Rodriguez. The Dodger inner defense remained alert for a play at the plate. Guidry's bunt gave them an opportunity. Reuss pounced on the ball and quickly threw to Yeager in order to force Watson. Reuss ended the inning without surrendering a run when he got Randolph to bounce out to Garvey.

Guidry was awesome when the Dodgers came up. He struck out the side with a dazzling display of fastballs, that left Cey, Baker and Guerrero all swinging. It gave him six strikeouts, the last four in succession. He appeared as strong as he did in the opening game in New York.

Reuss was determined to keep pace. He got Milbourne on a grounder to start the fifth inning. Winfield snapped his slump by lining a single to left. It was his first hit in 16 tries! Surprisingly, Winfield asked for time with a request to keep the ball as a souvenir. Reuss looked puzzled but surrendered the ball. He then concentrated on Jackson, who hit into an inning-ending double play.

The Dodgers were still ineffective at the plate. Yeager popped out. Thomas struck out to become Guidry's seventh victim. Reuss collected a walk on a full count pitch but died on the basepaths as Rodriguez threw out Lopes.

Jerry Reuss says it all after getting final out in ninth inning.

Game 5	1	2	3	4	5	6	7	8	9	Total
New York	0	1	0	0	0	0	0	0	0	1
Los Angeles	0	0	0	0	0	0	2	0	x	2

Reuss had an easy inning in the sixth. He turned back the Yanks in order for the first time since the opening inning, putting out Watson, Piniella and Cerone. Yet, the Dodgers remained powerless. After Russell skied out, Guidry recorded his eighth strikeout–against Garvey. He completed the inning when Cey grounded out to Rodriguez.

The seventh inning was another easy one for Reuss. He got Rodriguez on a grounder, struck out Guidry and made Randolph bounce to Russell. By this time Guidry had already gone six innings and there wasn't anyone warming up in the Yankee bullpen. It didn't seem necessary. As Guidry whiffed Baker at the start of the inning, it was his ninth strikeout, the most for any pitcher in the Series. Then Guidry, who started off Guerrero with a strike, hung a slider. Guerrero jumped on it. The ball went sailing into the left center field pavillion to tie the game at

The Dodger hopes were alive now. Fans showered the stadium with paper as Guidry began rubbing a new ball in his hands. Yeager stepped into the batter's box. He had cracked a homer off Guidry in the opener. Could it happen again? Guidry fooled him with several sliders and got him in the hole with a 1–2 count. Then he tried to throw a fastball past Yeager. Yeager swung and drilled a shot into the left field stands for a home run that sent the Dodgers into a 2–1 lead. The fans were giddy by now. They couldn't have cared less that Guidry retired Thomas and Reuss to end the inning.

It was strictly Reuss' game now. He seemed to grow stronger as he pitched the eighth. The crowd yelled as he got Milbourne on an infield tap and struck out Winfield and Jackson on a harmless fly to Baker. Reuss had retired eleven Yankees in a row. There were only three more left!

Gossage came in to finish the game. Lopes worked him for a walk. Russell, attempting to bunt, popped to Watson. Garvey flied to Piniella, who had shifted to right, for the second out. Cey, who led all batters with nine runs batted in, was hoping to add to his total but he never got the chance. Gossage's first pitch, a fast ball that was timed at 94 MPH, struck Cey with a sickening thud on the left side of his head. He dropped to the ground as a hush fell over Dodger Stadium. Although he didn't lose consciousness, Cey remained on the ground for several minutes. He finally left the field to thunderous applause as Landreaux went in to run for him. Lopes and Landreaux then executed a double steal, but Baker left them stranded by grounding out.

All eyes were on Reuss. If he could repel the Yankees once more the Dodgers would get the upper hand in the Series for the first time. He got Watson to ground out for the first out. However, Piniella touched him for a single and the tying run was on. It was the first hit Reuss had yielded since the fifth inning. Cerone flied out, leaving it up to Rodriguez, who was no match for Reuss. Reuss fanned him on three pitches, sending the Dodgers and their fans into pandemonium. Who would have dreamed that the Dodgers would snap back with three straight victories?

Reuss was a lot more confident following his third kayo in the opener.

"I knew if we held them close and somebody gets me a run or two, I'm going to get them," said Reuss. "I was more embarrassed than mad at myself after the game in New York, because I wasn't throwing the way I did during the season. If I throw more than 10 or 12 curveballs in any game, that's a lot for me. I made up my mind out here in my ballpark I was going to pitch my way. If they were going to beat me, it was going to be with my best pitch.

"Before we started the Series, we went over the scouting reports in detail, but today I finally got to the point where I was going to pitch my kind of ball game. I didn't totally disregard the scouting report, but I went with my fastball and concentrated on keeping it down, which I didn't do well enough in New York. That and an extra day's rest really helped me. It made a big difference in the eighth and ninth innings. Of the 98 pitches that I threw, 93 or 94 were fastballs."

The one fastball that all the Dodger players were most concerned about was the one that hit Cey. He had remained in the trainer's room for a long time. The team physician, Dr. Frank Jobe, examined him and reported that the preliminary diagnosis was that he'd suffered a concussion. By now, Cey's wife, Fran, had joined him. Dr. Jobe sent them both to the hospital in an ambulance for x-rays. Fortunately, the x-rays were negative and Cey was allowed to go home. His wife was told to let him sleep but to wake him every two hours to check his alertness.

"He'll play in New York," smiled Fran, "unless he doesn't remember his name. I think he's got that down pat."

Before he left, Gossage stopped by the Dodger clubhouse to see how Cey was. When he was told that Cey would be all right relief showed on his face.

"I just wanted to make sure he was O.K.," said Gossage. "If he'd hit me in the face with a line drive, he'd be in to see me. I was just aiming it down the middle of the plate and the ball got away from me. It was headed right for his head, and he didn't have any time to react. I heard it hit the helmet. If he hadn't had a helmet on, he might be dead. I kept saying, 'get up, get up.'

"There was nothing more I could do. I didn't want to get upset, that's why I didn't go down near the plate to see him. It's scary, but thank God I didn't hit him in the face. Lopes stopped by the mound on his way to second to tell me that the ball had just about gotten all of Cey's helmet. It sounded like hitting a hollow log."

Hollow is how the Yankees felt after losing all three games in Los Angeles. It was back to Broadway. . . .

Davey Lopes walked in final turn at bat in eighth inning.

GAME SIX

On Monday morning, with the Dodgers already in New York, Cey was being examined by a neurosurgeon. Pronounced sound, he boarded a plane later that afternoon to join the rest of his teammates. He was determined to be part of the Dodger miracle of 1981. A steady rain cancelled the workout scheduled for later that afternoon. Since the forecast was for more rain on Tuesday, Commissioner Bowie Kuhn announced that the sixth game would be postponed until Wednesday night. It was a break Cey hadn't expected.

"I had some light-headedness, dizziness," he said. "I had decided against going to the park, dressing easy or even trying to workout. I was relieved when it was called off. I did have a chance to see some replays of the beaning. Since I knew what the outcome was, I felt a little better about seeing them. All I can tell you is that I feel extremely fortunate to be standing here.

"It's pretty difficult to get out of the way of any baseball that takes off when it's going 94 MPH. I was trying to stay in on the pitch as long as I could. When I decided to get out of the way, the ball just followed me, like a magnet. I remember hitting the ground in slow motion. At least it felt like slow motion. I was in kind of a stupor, in another world. I don't remember a lot until somebody got to the plate. I asked the first question: 'What do I look like? Am I all right?' I told them, 'I feel like I'm incoherent. I understand all the questions you're asking me.'

"Later, I was being treated in the trainer's room and watched the last inning of the game on TV Then they sent me to the hospital, where they made the first tests. Once they determined there was no fracture, the greatest danger was a blood clot. Sunday night, I went home and talked it out with my wife, Fran. I had come to grips with reality. I don't take great plunges int religion to explain things like that. But I decided that somebody somewhere must be testing me. I don't know why.

"I don't go around blaming God for the things that happened to me this year. But somewhere in the great design for this year, I am being tee It's strange what turns your life can take. Sunday, the only thing that mattered was playing that game. Today, the only thing that matters is that I'm sitting here—no blood clot, no fractured skull. Your priorities change. You realize how your whole world can change in one instant.

"The brain scan eliminated the worst fears, physically. Now, emotionally where am I? Well, I can't feel that I am all right there. Thinking it through with my wife, I came to grips with my life and my priorities. My health became No. 1. Am I afraid to bat? I don't believe so. It's part of my professional risk. I don't live in fear of the plate. If I did, I could never play the game. If I can't sustain the workout before the game, I won't go out there. Hopefully, when I go to bat for the first time, I'll handle it."

A sense of quiet confidence prevailed among the Dodger players before Cey even got to New York. They were loose. Instead of turning away interviews, they made themselves accessible to the hundreds of media people covering the fall classic. In fact, while the Yankees were enroute to New York, Lasorda brought some of his players with him to a press conference. Among others, he had Scioscia, Garvey and Johnstone with him.

"I'm disappointed at not playing on Wednesday night," began Scioscia, "but Yeager has started against lefthanders all year. That's what the Yankees are throwing, and if I were the manager, I'd do the same thing. Did I say that okay, Tommy?"

Lasorda couldn)t help but laugh. He spoke first about Garvey.

"Steve Garvey is as outstanding a young man as I've ever known. No one gives more to his job. I've never seen him do anything to hurt anybody. The only time he's been disliked here is by people who were jealous of him."

Next Lasorda talked about Johnstone.

"He's a winner. The problem is finding him. I'll say, 'Get Johnstone,' The coaches will ask, 'Where is he?' I don't know what part of the ballpark he warms up in, but when he gets to the plate in crucial situations, he's ready."

Someone asked Garvey if he would discuss the agility that is required to play first base. Garvey couldn't resist.

"It takes years of preparation," said Garvey. "Being a defensive back in the Big 10 helped. And then, I tell our infielders to keep the bad throws low. Scooping is one of my strengths. But seriously, it's high time this group won."

Johnstone took Garvey's comment further.

"Several guys on our team realize that this may be their last year in a Dodger uniform," added Johnstone. "They are out there winning not for the fans, or management, but for themselves. These are special people. Like Garvey said when we left here last week, down 0–2. We had the Yankees right where we wanted them."

How do players get along with Garvey, someone else wanted to know.

"To begin with," replied Johnstone," anybody who has plastic hair, who shaves with a hammer and chisel, is gonna have people say funny things about him. Here's a guy who has apple pie in his back pocket, butter melting in his mouth, an American flag on his car as he drives down the street. The thing is, he's the same person on the field as he is anywhere else. He's real. We get along great, which is an admission that could pull down my reputation. But someday he'll be president, I'll be his minister of defense, and together we'll take care of Cuba."

It was time for Lasorda to get serious.

"The turning point in this Series was Saturday's game," he said. "One week ago, we were still in Montreal, playing for the pennant, and our pitchers were short on rest. We'd been using a three-man rotation; but Saturday, we took a bit of a gamble. We started Bob Welch and although he didn't last very long, we won the game.

"It was crucial because it gave our three regular starters an extra day of rest. Now Hooton has five days off instead of three. And Fernando will have four days of rest instead of three if we're forced to play the seventh game. That's the biggest change in our fortunes, our pitching is finally rested."

When the Yankees arrived later Monday night, word had already reached New York that Steinbrenner had gotten into a fight with a couple of Los Angeles fans in the elevator of the hotel where the Yankees were staying. Steinbrenner had a cast on his left hand.

"The first guy recognized me," said Steinbrenner. "He said, 'Hey, you're Steinbrenner, right? You're going back to the animals in New York and you're taking your choke-up team with you.' I'd had a bellyful of comments like that, and I told him where to get off. At that point the guy swung a beer bottle and hit me on the side of the head. I knocked him down with a right hand. I'm not sure what happened next, but I know the other guy was swinging at me. I hit him with a left hand that felt like it loosened a couple of his teeth and knocked him off the elevator.

"I went down to the second floor to meet Cedric Tallis and Bill Bergersch for dinner. I guess I had some blood on my teeth and my hair was messed up because Cedric said, 'What the hell happened to you?' I said, 'I know you're not going to believe this." We then went to the lobby to notify hotel security. That really was the end of it because the security people couldn't find them.

"I'm aware that some people are saying this is another Steinbrenner trick to soup up his team. Some trick. How could I beat myself up like this? How is this going to soup up the team? If anything, I'm sure the team thinks it's humorous."

Indeed they did. The Yankee players made light of the incident. They've been subjected to their share of fights over the years, particularly those of ex-manager Billy Martin and the latest involving Jackson and Nettles ten days earlier in Oakland, which gave rise to such one liners as:

"I didn't punch that doggie, George did."

"Who's throwing out the first ball tomorrow night, Muhammad Ali?"

"Is organist Eddie Layton going to play the Rocky theme before tomorrow's game?"

"Does this mean we're going to bring Sugar Ray Robinson to spring training as an instructor?"

There was a much more serious moment the next day when someone telephoned the police with a bomb scare directed at Dusty Baker. He threatened to blow up the Dodger dugout if Baker started the game. The police bomb squad was immediately dispatched to Yankee Stadium. They combed the Dodger

Ron Cey miraculously started sixth game in New York.

Game 6	1	2	3	4	5	6	7	8	9	Total
Los Angeles	0	0	0	1	3	4	0	1	0	9
New York	0	0	1	0	0	1	0	0	0	2

Pedro Guerrero powers a base hit.

dugout for an hour looking for explosives but couldn't find any. Baker, who was hitting only .105 with two hits in 19 at-bats, was worried more about his sore right hand.

"What's the matter, don't they want me to play?" asked Baker. "The way I've been playing, maybe they don't. I don't want to say anything about my hand because I don't want anyone to think I was using it as an excuse for my poor performance. Nobody believes you anyway. The bomb threat doesn't bother me and I don't need any special bodyguards. I just want to get out there and play."

The one-day postponement was beneficial for a number of players. It was a question of who benefitted more, the Yankees or the Dodgers. Nettles, who didn't play in Los Angeles, had another day to rest his injured thumb. Cey certainly welcomed the postponement. If the game had been played as scheduled, Cey would have remained in the

dugout. He admitted feeling dizzy when he woke and dressed late Tuesday morning.

Both starting pitchers were satisfied with the postponement. Tommy John, who carried the Yanks' last hope and who had pitched two innings of relief Saturday, considered it a bonus. So, too, did Burt Hooton, who was matching pitches with John for the second time.

"I've advocated pitching on three days' rest all along. But doing it during the season, then trying to do so in the playoffs and the World Series is no easy matter," Reuss pointed out. "I felt really good the last time out, but there was just no zip on the ball. Now we're going to have an extra day of rest for me and Fernando, and that will make us extra tough."

The only remaining question was whether Cey would play. He deferred his decision until the pre-game workouts. Lasorda left the final decision up to his third baseman. Cey took some swings during batting practice and said he could make it. No one can ever say that Cey doesn't have courage.

Lopes opened the game with a harmless bouncer to Nettles. When Russell grounded to Randolph, it looked as if John had his good sinker going again. Garvey solved him with a single to center. Cey received an ovation his turn up. He didn't show any effects of his beaning and pulled a single to left field as Garvey stopped at second. Baker had a chance to get the Dodgers on the scoreboard first, but continued his slump with a fly ball to Jackson.

Randolph walked, leading off the game for the Yanks. With Mumphrey, who was back in the lineup after being benched up, Randolph stole second. Hooton bore down. He got Mumphrey and Winfield on fly balls and struck out Jackson on a 3–2 pitch to end the threat.

Guerrero drove Jackson deep for his fly ball as the Dodgers came up for the second time. Monday grounded out to Milbourne. When Yeager did the same thing, Milbourne threw the ball away for an error. In the end it wasn't too costly as Hooton bounced out to John. Hooton had an easy time when he went back to the mound, retiring Watson, Nettles and Cerone.

After Lopes grounded out to Nettles for the second straight time, Russell lined a single to right. When he tried to steal, however, he was thrown out. Mumphrey then caught Garvey's fly for the third out. Hooton got Milbourne and John without any trouble in the Yanks' third turn at bat. Then with two out, Randolph brought the crowd of 56,513 to its feet by belting a home run into the left field stands. Hooton was still looking for the third out when Mumphrey singled and Winfield walked. He finally got Jackson, to end the inning.

John struck out Cey at the start of the fourth stanza. Baker snapped his slump with a solid single to center. After Guerrero lined to Winfield, the bottom third of the Dodger order came alive. Monday singled as Baker raced to third. Then Yeager drilled a single left that scored Baker with the tying run. Hooton struck out, but it was a new ballgame for him too. He responded by getting Watson

on a ground ball when the Yankees came up. Nettles ripped a double to right field, and Hooton had to bear down again. He did so by striking out Cerone on three pitches. With two out and first base open, Lasorda instructed Hooton to walk Milbourne and pitch to John. Lemon countered with a surprise move. He told Bobby Murcer to bat for John. Murcer created a stir with a deep fly that Monday pulled down in right field for a third out.

Frazier came in to face the Dodgers in the fifth inning and was greeted with a single by Lopes. Russell sacrificed him to second. The Dodgers were playing for the go-ahead run. Garvey flied to Winfield for the second out. Everything was left up to Cey. He delivered. He slammed a hit past second that sent Lopes home and gave the Dodgers a 2–1 lead. Baker kept the inning going with a single to center as Cey reached third. Guerrero delivered both runners with a booming triple to left centerfield that stretched the Dodgers' lead to 4–1. Although Monday struck out, Hooton now had a three-run cushion to work with. The Yanks posed a mild threat when Randolph began the fifth inning with a double, but Hooton turned back Mumphrey, Winfield and Jackson without any problems.

Lemon brought Davis out of the bullpen to face the Dodgers in the sixth inning. He started out all right by striking out Yeager, but lost his control and walked both Hooton and Lopes. Russell scored Hooton with a single that gave the Dodgers a 5–1 lead and brought in Reuschel to replace Davis. Maintaining the pressure, Lopes and Russell surprised everyone by executing a double steal. Garvey was then passed intentionally to load the bases. Cey wasn't feeling quite right and Thomas batted for him. He forced Russell at third as Lopes scored. Nettles then bobbled Baker's grounder, and the Dodgers had the bases filled again. Guerrero came through once more with a single that scored both Garvey and Thomas for the third and fourth runs of the inning. He ran to second on the throw in to the plate. With first base open, Monday was walked intentionally. Yeager ended the uprising by grounding out.

That outbreak practically gave the Dodgers the game *and* the championship. Behind 8–1, the Yanks were demoralized. They couldn't come back now. Just to make sure, Lasorda injected some defensive changes for the last four innings. Thomas went to third, Guerrero shifted to right field and Landreaux played center. After Watson bounced out, Nettles got a hit. Rodriguez ran for him. A walk to Cerone and another to Milbourne sparked action in the Dodger bullpen. Gamble was announced as a pinch-hitter for Reuschel. Lasorda didn't want to take any chances. He brought in Howe to face the lefthand-hitting Gamble. Lemon countered by calling back Gamble and sending up Piniella instead. He gave the Yanks a flicker of hope with a single that scored Rodriguez as the bases remained loaded. But Howe removed all doubts by getting Randolph and Mumphrey.

Lemon made another pitching change, bringing in May to pitch the seventh. He struck out Howe but lost Lopes on four pitches, and then settled down by retiring Russell and Garvey. The Dodgers needed just nine more outs now. Howe got three quick ones by turning back Winfield, Jackson and Watson.

After Thomas and Baker were retired Guerrero continued to swing a hot bat. He belted a 2–1 pitch for a homer that gave the Dodgers a 9–2 bulge. No one noticed when Landreaux was called out on strikes. The champagne was cooling in the Dodger clubhouse. A single by Rodriguez made Howe work harder. He set down Cerone, Milbourne and Bobby Brown, who was batting for May. Just three more to go.

Dave LaRoche had a quick inning, probably because the Dodgers were already tasting champagne. He got Yeager on a fly and then fanned Howe and Lopes. The stadium was one-third empty when Randolph began the Yanks' final at-bat with a walk. Howe then struck out Mumphrey and got Winfield on a fly ball. Jackson alone stood between the Dodgers and their championship. He fizzled. Lopes delayed the inevitable by booting his grounder. Only Watson remained and Guerrero squeezed his fly ball for the third out. The champagne was ready and waiting. Los Angeles had fashioned a remarkable comeback to become the 1981 world champions.

The Dodger clubhouse wasn't as boisterous as it had been in Montreal when they clinched the pennant. The exultant players wanted to savor this one, their first crown in 16 years. Lasorda was doused with champagne and sprayed with shaving cream. He never resisted.

"This is the greatest thing that ever happened to me in baseball," he said. "These guys have given me a lifetime of thrills in one season. I've never said this before, but I always wished that if the good Lord ever let us win the World Series, it would be against the club that beat us twice. I'm the happiest man in the world. We're bringing the championship back to Los Angeles where it belongs."

It belonged, first, to the players. This was their victory.

"There really never has been a moment like it in my career," said Garvey. "It's my first, and it represents 25 years of time, sweat and sacrifice. I'll admit there were tears in my eyes tonight. The feeling after Sunday's game was that we had reached a moment of destiny in this World Series after coming back from being down, 0–2, for the third time in post-season play. It takes a special brand of character to do that. I think the rainout yesterday gave us a chance to pull together as a unit even more."

Guerrero, who shared the Most Valuable Player award with Cey and Yeager, has first base coach Manny Mota to thank for the honor.

"He had been telling me all along that I was hitting straight up instead of hitting down in a crouch as I did all season," said Guerrero. "Before the game tonight, Manny sat down with me at my locker for 10 or 15 minutes and reminded me to stay down and see the ball better. I saw it good all five times and hit it good all five times.

"When I came up to the big leagues with the Dodgers, my dream was to play every day and to play the Yankees in the World Series and win. I thank God for making this dream come true. Everybody was happy before the game; everybody was up. We said we wanted to party tonight. We didn't want it to go to a seventh game and take any chances."

The Big Dodger in the sky made sure. . . .

Steve Yeager lifts Steve Howe in air after the final out of the sixth game.

DAY BY DAY WITH THE DODGERS
1981

GAME NO.	DATE	OPP.	PITCHERS OF DODGERS	OPP.	W or L	SCORE	RECORD	POS.	GA/GB
1.	4/9	Hst.	VALENZUELA (1-0)	J. Niekro	W	2-0	1-0	T1	---
2.	4/11	Hst.	Hooton (1-0)	Sutton	W	7-4	2-0	1	1/2
3.	4/12	Hst.	Sutcliffe (1-0)	Ruhle	W	3-2	3-0	1	1
4.	4/13	at S.F.	Stewart (1-0)	Ripley	W	4-3	4-0	1	1
5	4/14	at S.F.	VALENZUELA (2-0)	Blue	W	7-1	5-0	1	1 1/2
6	4/15	at S.F.	Hooton (2-0)	Whitson	W	4-2	6-0	1	1 1/2
7	4/17	at S.D.	Howe (0-1)	Lollar	L	2-3 (10)	6-1	1	1 1/2
8	4/18	at S.D.	VALENZUELA (3-0)	Wise	W	2-0	7-1	1	2 1/2
9	4/19	at S.D.	Welch (1-0)	Curtis	W	6-1	8-1	1	3
10	4/20	at Hst	Hooton (3-0)	Andujar	W	5-2	9-1	1	3 1/2
11	4/21	at Hst.	REUSS (0-1)	KNEPPER	L	0-1	9-2	1	3 1/2
12	4/22	at Hst.	VALENZUELA (4-0)	Sutton	W	1-0	10-2	1	3 1/2
13	4/23	SD	Sutcliffe (2-0)	Wise	W	3-1	11-2	1	3 1/2
14	4/24	SD	Castillo (0-1)	Lucas	L	5-6	11-3	1	2 1/2
15	4/25	SD	Howe (1-1)	Littlefield	W	2-1(11)	12-3	1	2 1/2
16	4/26	SD	REUSS (1-1)	Lucas	W	3-2	13-3	1	4
17	4/27	SF	VALENZUELA (5-0)	Griffin	W	5-0	14-3	1	4 1/2
18	4/28	SF	Sutcliffe (2-1)	RIPLEY	L	1-6	14-4	1	4
19	4/29	SF	Welch (1-1)	Blue	L	2-3	14-5	1	3
20	5/1	at Mtl.	Castillo (0-2)	Lee	L	8-9(13)	14-6	1	2 1/2
21	5/2	at Mtl.	REUSS (2-1)	Sanderson	W	4-0	15-6	1	3 1/2
22	5/3	at Mtl.	VALENZUELA (6-0)	Gullickson	W	6-1(10)	16-6	1	4 1/2
23	5/4	at Mtl.	Sutcliffe (2-2)	Rogers	L	3-4	16-7	1	4
24	5/5	at Phl.	Castillo (0-3)	Lyle	L	7-8	16-8	1	3 1/2
25	5/6	at Phl.	HOOTON (4-0)	Espinosa	W	2-1	17-8	1	3 1/2
26	5/7	at Phl.	REUSS (3-1)	Bystrom	W	2-1	18-8	1	4
27	5/8	at NY	VALENZUELA (7-0)	Scott	W	1-0	19-8	1	4
28	5/9	at NY	Castillo (0-4)	Allen	L	4-7	19-9	1	4
29	5/10	at NY	Welch (2-1)	Jones	W	5-3	20-9	1	4 1/2
30	5/12	Mtl.	Hooton (5-0)	Burris	W	5-0	21-9	1	4
31	5/13	Mtl.	Howe (2-1)	Fryman	W	8-6	22-9	1	5
32	5/14	Mtl.	VALENZUELA (8-0)	Ratzer	W	3-2	23-9	1	5 1/2
33	5/15	NY	Howe (3-1)	Allen	W	6-5	24-9	1	5 1/2
34	5/16	NY	HOOTON (6-0)	Roberts	W	9-0	25-9	1	5 1/2
35	5/17	NY	REUSS (4-1)	Zachry	W	6-1	26-9	1	5 1/2
36	5/18	Phl.	Valenzuela (8-1)	Bystrom	L	0-4	26-10	1	5
37	5/19	Phl.	Welch (2-2)	RUTHVEN	L	3-2	26-11	1	4
38	5/20	Phl.	Howe (4-1)	McGraw	W	3-2(10)	27-11	1	4
39	5/22	at Cin.	Stewart (2-0)	Bair	W	4-2(12)	28-11	1	5 1/2
40	5/23	at Cin.	Stewart (3-0)	Moskau	W	9-6(10)	29-11	1	6 1/2
41	5/24	at Cin.	Welch (2-3)	Moskau	L	2-3	29-12	1	
42	5/24	at Cin.	Castillo (1-4)	Berenyi	W	10-3	30-12	1	6 1/2
43	5/25	at Atl.	Hooton (7-0)	Walk	W	7-1	31-12	1	6 1/2
	5/26	at Atl.	-------------	--------	-	RAINED	OUT		
44	5/27	at Atl.	Howe (4-2)	Camp	L	2-3	31-13	1	5 1/2
45	5/28	at Atl.	Valenzuela (8-2)	Perry	L	4-9	31-14	1	4 1/2
46	5/29	Cin.	Welch (3-3)	LaCoss	W	5-2	32-14	1	5 1/2
47	5/30	Cin.	Hooton (7-1)	Pastore	L	1-9	32-15	1	4 1/2
48	5/31	Cin	Goltz (1-0)	Soto	W	16-4	33-15	1	5 1/2
49	6/1	Atl.	VALENZUELA (9-2)	Boggs	W	5-2	34-15	1	5 1/2
50	6/2	Atl.	Stewart (3-1)	Perry	L	1-3(10)	34-16	1	5 1/2
51	6/3	Atl.	Hooton (7-2)	P. Niekro	L	2-4	34-17	1	4 1/2
52	6/5	at Chi.	Reuss (4-2)	Reuschel	L	3-4	34-18	1	3 1/2

GAME NO.	DATE	OPP.	PITCHERS OF RECORD DODGERS	OPP.	W or L	SCORE	RECORDS	POS.	GA/GB
53	6/6	at Chi.	Valenzuela (9-3)	McGlothen	L	5-11	34-19	1	2 1/2
54	6/7	at Chi.	WELCH (4-3)	Martz	W	7-0	35-19	1	2 1/2
55	6/9	at St.L.	Hooton (7-3)	B. Forsch	L	1-6	35-20	1	1 1/2
56	6/10	at St.L.	REUSS (5-2)	Sorensen	W	4-1	36-20	1	1 1/2
57	6/11	at St.L.	Valenzuela (9-4)	Martinez	L	1-2	36-21	1	1/2
			END OF FIRST HALF						
58	8/10	Cin.	Reuss (6-2)	Pastore	W	4-0	1-0	T1	------
59	8/11	Cin.	Forster (0-1)	Brown	L	6-7	1-1	T2	1
60	8/12	Cin.	Stewart (4-1)	Seaver	W	8-5	2-1	T2	1
61	8/13	Atl.	Hooton (7-4)	Boggs	L	1-9	2-2	T2	2
62	8/14	Atl.	Goltz (2-0)	Montefusco	W	5-0	3-2	T2	1
63	8/15	Atl.	Reuss (6-3)	Bedrosian	L	4-6	3-3	T3	2
64	8/16	Atl.	Niedenfuer (1-0)	Bedrosian	W	6-5	4-3	T3	1 1/2
65	8/17	at Chi.	Welch (4-4)	BIRD	L	1-3	4-4	T3	1 1/2
66	8/18	at Chi.	HOOTON (8-4)	M. Griffin	W	5-0	5-4	T3	1
67	8/19	at Chi.	Goltz (2-1)	Krikow	L	3-4	5-5	T4	2
68	8/21	at St.L.	REUSS (7-3)	Andujar	W	4-0	6-5	T4	1
69	8/22	at St.L.	Valenzuela (10-4)	B. Forsch	W	3-2	7-5	T2	1/2
70	8/23	at St.L.	Welch (4-5)	Shirley	L	7-11	7-6	T2	1 1/2
71	8/24	at Pitt.	HOOTON (9-4)	O. Jones	W	3-0	8-6	2	1/2
72	8/25	at Pitt.	Pena (1-0)	Tekulve	W	9-7(11)	9-6	2	1/2
73	8/26	at Pitt.	Reuss (8-3)	Rhoden	W	16-6	10-6	2	1/2
74	8/27	Chi.	VALENZUELA (11-4)	Martz	W	6-0	11-6	T1	------
75	8/28	Chi.	Welch (5-5)	Krukow	W	6-1	12-6	1	1
76	8/29	Chi.	Hooton (9-5)	M. Griffin	L	1-3	12-7	1	1
77	8/30	Chi.	Goltz (2-2)	Bird	L	1-2	12-8	T1	------
78	8/31	Pitt.	Stewart (4-2)	O. Jones	L	4-5(10)	12-9	T3	1
79	9/1	Pitt.	Niedenfuer (2-0)	O. Jones	W	3-2(14)	13-9	3	1
80	9/2	Pitt.	Welch (6-5)	Long	W	6-2	14-9	2	1
81	9/3	St.L.	Howe (4-2)	Littell	L	3-5	14-10	3	2
82	9/4	St.L.	Goltz (2-3)	Martin	L	2-7	14-11	3	3
83	9/5	St.L.	Niedenfuer (3-0)	Kaat	W	4-3(11)	15-11	3	3
84	9/6	St.L	VALENZUELA (12-4)	B. Forsch	W	5-0	16-11	3	2
85	9/7	SF	Welch (7-5)	Whitson	W	5-1	17-11	2	2
86	9/8	SF	Hooton (10-5)	Alexander	W	4-0	18-11	2	1
87	9/9	SF	Niedenfuer (3-1)	Minton	L	3-6(11)	18-12	2	1
88	9/11	at Cin.	Pena (1-1)	Price	L	2-3(10)	18-13	2	2
89	9/12	at Cin.	Power (0-1)	LaCoss	L	5-6(11)	18-14	3	3
90	9/13	at Cin.	Castillo (2-4)	Pastore	W	4-2	19-14	2	3
91	9/14	at SD	Power (1-1)	Show	W	10-5	20-14	2	2
92	9/15	at SD	Goltz (2-4)	Eichelberger	L	2-8	20-15	2	2
93	9/16	Atl.	Reuss (9-3)	Perry	W	3-2	21-15	2	2
94	9/17	Atl.	VALENZUELA (13-4)	R. Mahler	W	2-0	22-15	2	2
95	9/18	Cin.	Stewart (4-3)	Price	L	4-5	22-16	2	2
96	9/19	Cin.	Hooton (10-6)	Edelen	L	3-7	22-17	3	3
97	9/20	Cin.	Power (1-2)	SOTO	L	1-5	22-18	3	4
98	9/22	at SF	Valenzuela (13-5)	Whitson	L	2-5	22-19	4	5
99	9/23	at SF	Goltz (2-5)	Lavelle	L	4-8	22-20	4	5
100	9/24	at SF	WELCH (8-5)	T. Griffin	W	7-3	23-20	4	5
101	9/25	at Hst.	HOOTON (11-6)	Ruhle	W	3-0	24-20	4	4
102	9/26	at Hst.	Power (1-3)	RYAN	L	0-5	24-21	4	5
103	9/27	at Hst.	Valenzuela (13-6)	SUTTON	L	1-4	24-22	4	6
104	9/28	at Atl.	Reuss (9-4)	R. Mahler	L	1-2	24-23	4	7
105	9/29	at Atl.	Howe (5-3)	Garber	W	5-3	25-23	4	6
106	9/30	SD	Goltz (2/6)	Boone	L	0-2	25-24	4	6
107	10/1	SD	Valenzuela (13-7)	Kuhualua	L	0-1	25-25	4	7
108	10/2	Hst.	REUSS (10-4)	Sutton	W	6-1	26-25	4	6
109	10/3	Hst.	Welch (9-6)	J. Niekro	W	7-2	27-25	4	5
110	10/4	Hst.	Goltz (2-7)	Smith	L	3-5	27-26	4	6

187